SHEPHERD OF THE HILLS
A BIOGRAPHY OF
TOMMY JONES OF YNYSYBWL
1901-1984

SHEPHERD OF THE HILLS
Copyright © Diana Wilson 2011

All Rights Reserved

No part of this book may be reproduced in any form,
by photocopying or by any electronic or mechanical means,
including information storage or retrieval systems,
without permission in writing from both the copyright
owner and the publisher of this book.

ISBN 978-0-9557858-1-8

First Published 2011

DEDICATION

I would like to dedicate this book to my husband, Ken; my children Beverley, Nicola, Karen and Helen; my grandchildren Richard, Thomas, Luke, Jamie Darren, Katy and Laura, Megan and Josh; my great grandchildren, Courtney, Morgan, Dewi-John, Caru Beth and Callie Jayne and all future great grandchildren. You have all given me such joy throughout my life, for which I remain eternally grateful.

To my sisters, Nancy and Llinos. I have been so lucky to have such wonderful sisters, who have been supportive to me all through my life. You are not only my sisters, but my best friends.

CONTENTS

Acknowledgements

Foreword

ACKNOWLEDGEMENTS

I wish to acknowledge the support and help of the following:

My Uncle Dave and Aunty Marjorie in Scotland and my Aunty Joan in Ferndale, for believing in me and encouraging me to carry on writing even when times got difficult.

My cousin Audrey Williams, who has given a lot of her time and expertise in proof-reading my book and making it grammatically correct.

My cousin Dr Peter Brooks for his unwavering patience, having read, and amended numerous versions of the book, edited the photographic images and constructed the files ready for the printers. He has not only encouraged me, but given me the benefit of his own experience in writing and publishing.

Lloyd Coombes for his contribution and helping me to relive some wonderful memories. Thank you Lloyd for the help you gave Mam and Dad over the years. You were always regarded as "one of the family".

Without the help I have received from all these lovely people, this book would never have been written and I feel that would have been a sad loss.

FOREWORD

This is a true story, part of which was written by my father, Tommy Jones, several years ago. He wanted to record aspects of his life which he felt were important to him and perhaps of interest to other people. He wanted to describe how he discovered ways of training his sheepdogs and how this led to the making of the film 'Sheep Dog' in 1936 – a short film which depicted a day in the life of a shepherd. The film had its premiere at the Odeon Theatre, Leicester Square. At the time it was acclaimed as the best nature film ever made.

In advertising material Dad was described as 'The Welsh Wonder Shepherd' and his dog, Scott, was referred to as 'the cleverest dog in the World' in the 'Illustrated Magazine' of April 29th, 1939.

Unfortunately, Dad died before completing the book. I promised him that I would do so and although it has taken me many years, I hope I have finally given it the justice it deserves.

I felt it was important to give as complete a picture of Dad's life from the very beginning until the end. What follows, therefore, is essentially a biography of a man from humble beginnings in Ynysybwl who, for a short time, achieved international fame.

CHAPTER 1

EARLY YEARS

THE BEGINNING

Life began in 1901 in a terraced house in the mining village of Ynysybwl. It was not an easy beginning for my father, Thomas Jones.

At the time of his birth his mother, Mary Morgan, was 19 years old. She had been born in Cymmer, Porth, in the Rhondda Valley, in 1882. Her mother had died when Mary was a young child. Her father re-married a woman who had two children of her own. Mary's relationship with her step-mother was not to be a good one. She was treated badly; when she was just 12 years old, in order to escape from a life of drudgery and cruelty, she ran away, eventually arriving in Cardiff. It is believed that she walked all the way.

Mary had a sister, Nancy, who had recently married and moved to Ynysybwl. Her husband was a gentle and kind man who, on hearing of Mary's disappearance, went in search of her and found her in Cardiff. He brought her home to live with them in Ynysybwl. Mary stayed with them for a year. However Mary and Nancy did not have a close sisterly relationship. Nancy was expecting her first child and didn't feel she could cope with looking after Mary as well as her own family. It was decided that they should look for somewhere for Mary to work in service. The result was that she moved to West Wales to live on a farm, where she worked as a maid. Here she remained until she was 18 years old.

In October, 1900, Mary became pregnant. It is believed that the father of her child was the son of her employer, although there does not appear to be any conclusive evidence of this. It is only through conversations that Mary had with various members of her family that this emerged. As was so often the case in these years, the pregnancy was concealed as much as possible. Mary was sent home to return to live with Nancy and her husband and it was in their home that Dad was born in July 1901.

Nancy's husband took on the role of father and gave him his name, Thomas Jones. He and Nancy had had three daughters, one of whom died at an early age; the youngest child was only 6 months old when Dad was born. Although he was known as Thomas Jones, my father had never been officially adopted. The name on his birth certificate was Thomas Morgan. His mother's name was recorded as Mary Morgan and father recorded as 'unknown'.

Dads birth mother, Mary, met and married Evan Davies in 1903 and had a further 12 children. They lived at the opposite end of the same terrace where Dad was brought up by Nancy and Thomas Jones.

Mary always maintained that she loved him dearly, but was not allowed to acknowledge Dad as her son; Nancy felt it was not appropriate because she wanted him to be brought up as part of her family. Oblivious to the circumstances surrounding his birth, Dad's memories of his early childhood were happy ones in which he felt loved and secure. He talked very fondly of his mother and father and his sisters. He never had any reason to doubt that he was not the son of Nancy and Thomas. He grew up believing that Mary was his maternal aunt, and her children his cousins.

Although he lived in the same street as his birth mother and her family, he had very limited contact with them.

He attended the local village school, Trerobart. He was a very pretty child who, it appears, became quite a favourite of the teacher.

SCHOOLDAYS

Dad often reminisced about his schooldays. Most people in the village at that time spoke both Welsh and English, as did Dad. Although education was seen as important, for the majority of people in the South Wales valleys at this time, families often found themselves more concerned with issues of daily existence.

One of Dad's favourite tales was of being in school with boys who lived in the same street as him. One of the boys, Billy, was a particularly close friend of Dad. His mother saw little point in education. She, herself, was illiterate, and this was true of all the other occupants of the household. At the end of the year, the school reports were sent home with the pupils.

This lad had not done well and was described by Dad as being 'bottom of the class'. He didn't want his mother and father to know this. This didn't pose much of a problem, because he knew that no-one in the house would be able to read the report. He rushed home from school, as he had in previous years, holding the report in his hand and shouting excitedly to his unassuming mother "Look Mam, top of the class again!" His mother, having no reason to disbelieve him, proudly took the report around to the neighbours, telling them that her son had come top of the class again. It appears that the neighbours were kindly folk, who went along wholeheartedly with her, not wanting to deflate the enormous feeling of pride she held.

Billy had a particularly tough and strict father. He worked in the colliery and was said to have ruled the household with a rod of iron. He would not tolerate misbehaviour from any of the children, who would suffer his wrath should they disobey him. His way of punishing the children was to whip them with his leather belt, which he always wore around his waist. Dad remembered being absolutely terrified of him, and although he spent a lot of time in the house with the boys, he always made sure that he left before their father returned home from work just in case he was in a bad mood.

All of the children were expected to find some sort of job; a newspaper round or delivering groceries to bring in some income. Any money earned had to be handed over immediately to their father. One day Billy had been paid his usual wage for delivering papers for the local newsagent. He was so excited about having his own money that he decided he would buy his mother a present. He went into the local drapers shop and bought some hair clips. As he came out of the shop with his pay, he met up with some friends. Proudly showing them his wages, they set about persuading him to buy some sweets. Billy, being very easily led, and of a generous nature, decided that he would buy a half-penneth worth. Having parted with a little of his wages, temptation took over. For weeks he had looked longingly in a draper's shop window at a belt, with a snake fastening. He thought how it would make a lovely present for his father. He decided he would buy it. Later, showing it off to all his friends he became really excited and couldn't wait to go home to show his mother and father. Billy, not being the brightest of boys, did not really understand how money worked. Every time he had paid for something and was given change, he thought he was having more money than he had spent.

Billy's pleasure was short-lived. On arriving home his father asked him where his money was. Billy had already given his mother the hair clips that he had bought for her and had shown her the belt. She knew that there was trouble ahead, and looked very anxious. Billy, with a smile from ear to ear, told his father that he had bought him a present and proceeded to show him the belt. He could see his father was not impressed and having suffered his father's wrath, he knew he was in for a beating. Dad said that he rose from his chair, his face crimson with rage. He took his belt off and told Billy to get upstairs. That was enough for Dad and he high-tailed it out of the back door.

He was not seen for the rest of that day, but later on that evening Dad caught a glimpse of him up in his bedroom window. His eyes were red and swollen. Dad shouted up to ask him what was the matter, and without another word, he pulled his trousers down and there, almost like a tattoo, was a bruise, the shape of a snake clearly visible on his backside. Billy never spent his pay again.

When Dad related these stories about his schooldays he maintained that there were very few children in the class who could remotely be called bright. He included himself in this category and said that it was commonplace for the whole class to copy each other's work. He said there were a few who seemed to be brighter than the rest of them, so they would try to copy off one whom they considered would be most likely to get the right answer. This worked if they picked the right one, but some of the time that wasn't the case and if the one they copied from had the answer wrong, then the whole class would have it wrong.

One other aspect of school life always intrigued Dad. He had vivid memories of two men who would come to the school once a year. He was brought out from the classroom into the school yard to see them. He was never told who they were, or why they wanted to see him. Only in adulthood, when he discovered that he was not Nancy's son, came the realisation that these were probably members of his birth father's family, and possibly one of them might even have been his father. This memory worried him to the end of his days. He always felt as if a piece of a jigsaw was missing in his life. He used to say 'If only I knew what he looked like.

Life for Dad changed dramatically when he was four years old. His step-father, Thomas Jones, became ill with Tuberculosis and died. Nancy was left with four children (including Dad) to bring up on her own. Inevitably, life became extremely hard for her. She re-married within a short time. Her second husband was a first cousin of her first husband. He is said to have been a very violent man, and a drunkard. Most of the household income was spent on drink. There were four sons from this marriage each born in quick succession. Dad said that this man obviously didn't like children and the once happy home that he was born into became a house of misery for them all.

HIS FIRST JOB

CRIBYNDU

In 1914, when he was just 13 years old, Dad left home. He was offered a job on a farm, Cribyndu, in Ynysybwl. He never forgot his first encounter with the farmer, who was to be his employer. When the morning arrived for him to start work he was nervous and his stomach was churning as he walked up to the farm. On the steps of the barn stood a tall man, slight and with a long beard. Dad thought he was the living image of Jesus as he had always imagined him. This was Dewi Williams, one of five bachelor brothers who lived on the farm. He was a kind and gentle soul. His first words to Dad were "Have you seen the showering stars?" Dad never forgot those words. He felt that Dewi was a man full of compassion and was trying to make their first introduction as easy as he could. He later learned that Dewi had always been very interested in astronomy and observing the night sky; the hope of seeing a shooting star was something that gave him a real thrill.

Dad's wages were negotiated between his mother and Dewi. He was to be paid two shillings and sixpence a week. He was expected to start work at half past five in the morning and work until dusk; in the summer this could mean finishing at 10.30pm. He would live in the farmhouse and his meals would be provided.

A typical day's work meant rising at 5.30am, then going to the stable to feed the pony. From there he would go to the cowshed, throw hay down from the loft above for the eighteen cows and the half a dozen calves. He would then clean out under the cows. By this time, his boss would arrive.

Dad would milk seven of the cows and then walk to the next farm, which was some three quarters of a mile away, to collect their surplus milk, - usually about five gallons. This would be taken back to the cowshed where his boss carefully measured it, and added it to his own. Then came breakfast. The meals at Cribyndu never varied. Bacon for breakfast, home cured with hardly a streak of lean in the middle of the fat. The same bacon was served up cold for lunch, together with some boiled potatoes and yet again for supper. Dad said there was no point in complaining - you ate it or starved!

After breakfast he would take the milk down to the village with the horse and milk float. For the rest of the day he was expected to do anything that was asked of him. He always said that in those days, as a worker, you were owned 'body and soul' by your employer; you had no life of your own; you woke in the morning, worked hard all day, until you were glad to go to bed in the night. There was no 'fun'.

HIS FIRST ATTEMPT AT TRAINING

Dad's first interest in sheepdogs came when he listened to a story being told in school about a Scottish shepherd. The shepherd had a dog called 'Sirrie'. He was bringing 300 lambs home to shelter from the hills, when it became so dark that visibility was very poor and he lost them. When he awoke in the morning, the 300 lambs were outside his door; Sirrie had collected them on his own during the night. The impact this story had on Dad was tremendous. He thought about that shepherd and his dog constantly. He couldn't comprehend how a dog could do such a thing. He longed from that day to own a dog of his own and one that could match Sirrie.

His employer at Cribyndu had a dog called Rock. When Dad took the milk down in the mornings, Rock would follow him. He was a big strong dog, and Dad became very fond of him. At the top of High Street in Ynysybwl, there was a dog who really thought he was 'King of the Road'. He would challenge every dog he saw. Every day he would come tearing out of the house just as Dad and Rock were passing with the horse and cart. Rock never retaliated and appeared to be afraid of him. As they were going back up the farm lane, Dad thought "One day, I'm going to teach you a lesson you won't forget." He began to get Rock into training.

Near Cribyndu was a Mansion - 'Y Glog'. Here were the kennels where the hounds belonging to the local hunt were kept. Every day, dead animals were brought from neighbouring farms to be used to feed the hounds. The meat would be hung on spikes outside the kennels. Every morning, when Dad passed through the yard, he would take a piece of meat back for Rock. Before the end of milking, he would take a 'jack' of milk out and hide it - his employer would not have taken kindly to this. When he came home from taking the milk down to the village, he would prepare Rock's breakfast, - the meat and milk. He knew if he had any hope of winning his fight with this bully, Rock had to be in a good condition.

He fed him for weeks and finally the day arrived. Rock jumped on the cart with Dad and off they trotted. As they approached the house where the dog lived, out he came, barking, growling and throwing out his challenge to Rock. Dad threw Rock on top of the dog. A vicious fight took place. Eventually Rock emerged the winner. The dog had finally given in and run home with his tail between his legs. The dog never challenged again. Whenever they passed the house, he would just lie down and put his head on one side.

There were no sheep kept on Cribyndu, but every autumn they would have 200 tack lambs to winter for another farmer. Dad used to love seeing them arrive, the shepherds on their horses, working their dogs and bringing this huge flock effortlessly up the mountain. There were Welsh, English and Scottish shepherds, all of whom worked for the Powell Duffryn Coal Company. They were real 'old timers' with long heavy beards. Amongst them was 'Bamford the Maindy' who was a smart little man; 'David Phillips, Bedlwyn' who was about seventeen stone, a huge man who used to ride an old cart-horse. There was 'David Davies, Bwllfa'; a small man, rough and tough. He only had one arm but a ring fixed in the stump of his other arm, into which he would put his stick. Dad said he didn't know how he managed to catch the sheep, because he was a very 'stiff' man and not at all agile, but somehow or other he did. Then there was John Mathews. He was a very good-looking man, about 6 ft. tall and about 16 to 17 stone, very intelligent; Dad used to love talking to him. Jim Gordon was a Scottish shepherd, again a fine figure of a man, about 5ft. 10 ins tall and about 17 stone; a very wild and excitable character.

Dewi had a dog called Terk. After the sheep arrived, Dad had some big ideas of trying to train him to work the sheep, but Dewi saw Dad and stopped him. Dad never knew whether Dewi thought he would harm the sheep, or whether Dewi thought Dad was paid to do only certain work, which did not include working with the sheep.

Dad remained at Cribyndu Farm for a few years. He was never actually shown how to do any job, he simply had to watch and learn. However he never regretted working there because some of the men working at Cribyndu were skilled craftsmen and through watching them, when he had a spare moment, he learnt a great deal including the art of stone walling and hedging. These skills were to help him greatly when he eventually had his own farm.

After having a row with the housekeeper one day, he decided to leave Cribyndu. He asked the local colliery manager for a job. The Manager looked at Dad, who was only 4ft. 10 inches tall. Dad said he must have thought to himself "Well, look out- now the coal will come up!" At least he gave him a job.

DOWN THE MINES

LADY WINDSOR

On his first day working at the colliery Dad met with friends, collected his lamp from the lamp-room and made his way to the coal-face, descending the shaft in the cage. He would never forget the feeling he had as that cage slowly descended to the bottom of the shaft. He was petrified. It was pitch -black and the cage seemed to bang from side to side as it was lowered down.

There were six or seven boys working in the same district. In the morning, they would walk down an underground incline - about a mile or more to walk. He remembered the air was always warm. They would sweat profusely. His comment was "God only knows how miners used to work in such terrible conditions".

After walking about three or four hundred yards towards the coal-face the 'butties' (the colliers to whom the boys were allocated) would sit at a 'parting'. They would be here for about 15 to 20 minutes just to chat and rest. The boys would then go on up to the coal face, and there they would sit for a while cleaning their lamps. They would carry a clean piece of rag so that they could clean the inside of the glass. The old miners' lamps could be opened very easily and all they had to do was to the give the bottom of the lamp a sharp twist, and they would open.

Years later, when he was riding his horse on the top of a mountain, breathing in the fresh air and looking up to the heavens above, Dad thought how lucky he was to be alive. He and his colleagues could have been killed quite easily, being ignorant of the dangers of the environment in which they worked. He said he would picture the scene often, a row of lamps, all open, the naked lights on the floor, not a foot from the coal face.

Efforts were being made at this time, to improve the safety lamp. The Patterson lamp and later the Thomas and Williams lamp were developed. In Dad's view "By God, it was none too soon". Some of the boys later became firemen and bosses of one kind or another. He wondered whether they also thought how lucky they were to be alive.

As well as the problems associated with flammable gasses, there were other dangers. One activity which could so easily have resulted in death or serious injury was to ride in an empty tram. Each boy was in the charge of a man who was responsible for their safety. After most of the colliers had finished their work the boys were kept behind to fill the last tram and then they would run out, so that they could have a ride up the incline. There was always an empty tram behind the journey of coal, so that anything they wanted to take up to the colliery surface, could be carried in it - harnesses in need of repair, etc. The boys would jump into the last tram and ride up. If the rope had broken (which it did occasionally) it would have been instant death for them all; the tram would have been thrown off the road resulting in full trams of coal depositing their contents on them and probably causing a roof fall, burying them all.

Dad didn't work in the colliery for long. He said being a miner was like being a mole, hardly ever seeing daylight. It would be dark when he went to work in the morning and dark when he came home. Every time he came out of the cage, he would look up towards the mountain. It looked so appealing to him and he knew that that was where he belonged. He hated every minute of his work in the colliery. However, his experience of work in the colliery led to a life-long respect for the miners.

BLAENLLECHAU FARM

After leaving the Colliery, Dad went to work as a farmhand at Blaenllechau Farm. The Farm employed a few servants, a Bailiff, and Dad was a general farm labourer. There were a few maids who helped both with the house and with the milking.

It was here that Dad had some frightening experiences, which he related later in life, time and time again, to people who came to visit. It was said that the farmhouse was haunted. One of the first owners of the farm apparently was said to have had some unfortunate experience while living there, and was known to have a difficult temperament. He always said that when he died he would come back and haunt whoever lived there.

Dad said that one night he and another young lad, who had just started work there, had gone to bed. Everybody had been asleep for some time, when Dad awoke to hear the door knob on the bedroom door turning and the door opening. He got out of bed but there was no-one to be seen. He thought it must have been the wind and went back to bed. He then heard someone screaming downstairs. He got up and ran down to find all the servants in the hallway, all having been woken by the noise. As they stood there together they heard a noise as if chains were being dragged across the floor and then the door was blown open by a gust of wind which seemed to come from nowhere; the sound seemed to go out through the door.

They were all terrified as there was no logical explanation for what they had witnessed.

On another occasion a hurricane took the roof off the house. He always said that from that day there always seemed to be a problem with the roof and that several times the roof had blown off.

It was during the time that he was living at Blaenllechau that he met Mam, who was living with her parents in Wind Street, Blaenllechau.

This was 1928 and cars were very few and far between. The main form of transport was still horse and cart. Dad wanted to impress Mam, and asked her if she would go with him and a friend of his, who had a car, to Barry Island. As you can imagine, this was an offer that couldn't be turned down. He, his friend, his friend's girlfriend and Mam all got into the car. Dad, who had never driven anything apart from horses in his life, got behind the wheel. He did not want to admit to Mam that he had never driven before, or that he couldn't reverse, so whenever it became necessary to turn around, he would go to a place where he could turn the car without having to reverse.

Margaret Jane Thomas (Mam) c1929

He couldn't swim and didn't want Mam to know that either, (although she herself couldn't swim). They went into the sea, and Dad, pretending that he could swim, was lifting one arm above the water, whilst keeping one hand and foot still on the floor. I don't think that Mam was fooled, but they often laughed about it.

They married in 1930. Dad left Blaenllechau Farm and they moved to live with Mam's parents in Regent Street Ferndale.

TIRGWAIDD

HIS DREAM COMES TRUE

Dad's next move was to work at Tirgwaidd, a farm on Cefn Gwyngul, the hillside between Tylorstown and Llanwonno. He had heard that the tenant of Tirgwaidd was looking for a boy to work on the farm. He approached Mr. Richard Walters, to ask if he would take him on. Dad said when he arrived at Tirgwaidd he thought it was as if he was expected.

He started work for a weekly wage of seven shillings and sixpence. It was a wonderful place to live. There was always a "good table" with plenty to eat. But after just three weeks, he asked Mr Walters if he could leave. Here, in the narrow Rhondda Fach, he felt as if the mountains on each side of the valley rose as if they were reaching heaven. But the mountains appeared so high, and the valley so narrow, that he felt as if he was suffocating. His boss asked him to stay a little longer. "You'll get used to it" he said. He did and he was there for six very happy years.

At Tirgwaidd he had the care of two working horses and a cob mare used for shepherding. After milking the cows and feeding the horses he would go in for breakfast, when he would be given his orders for the day. It was at Tirgwaidd that Dad first started shepherding. He would ride on horseback down to the valley bottom to drive the sheep back up to the mountain, clearing the sheep from the main railway line and the roads.

At this time, Dad's sister, Maggie, was working as a maid at 'The Cefn', a farm in Ynysybwl. A bitch had just given birth to a litter of pups. They were all going to be drowned, but the bailiff gave one of the pups to Maggie and said "Take this pup to your brother - he will make a good dog". He knew little about dogs, but how true his words turned out to be. Maggie took the pup to Tirgwaidd, carrying him in her pocket. This was the first dog Dad had ever owned. There was nothing very pretty about him, but he fell in love with him straight away and maintained that this little bundle of fur was responsible for changing his life.

CHAPTER 2

OLD SCOTT

" Scott," a sheep-dog owned by Mr. Thomas Jones, of Ferndale, feeding a lamb near the Romilly Park, Barry, on Thursday.

Dad, when writing his rough notes for this book, wanted to emphasise the love he felt for his dog and the relationship that was formed between them. The following passage is taken from his manuscript and is presented here exactly as it was written:

"Scott, about you I want to write. As long as there are sheep dogs around, you will not be forgotten. I am going to try my best to remember all the wonderful things you did so that people for evermore will know how marvelous you were. The first day I remember anyone commenting on you was the day I was going up to the Dduallt Farm to help Ted Williams to do some hedging. Ted was a champion hedger. He taught me a lot about his trade, whilst I was with him. I had Scott with me. Ted said "send him around those sheep". I did, but there was no shape in him at all. Ted said "He's going to be a courser" I was really upset and disappointed. I could not blame you, Scott, as I myself didn't have a clue about training a dog. We both started from scratch.

As I have said, I had started to do some shepherding and noticed gradually that Scott was beginning to show some style with the sheep. He used to love coming with me and I noticed that right from the beginning, he would do little things which I had not asked of him, as if he was doing them out of his head. I started teaching him to carry things. In the winter time, I never used to go to the house until it was time to go to bed. During the evening, I used to stay in the stable, training Scott. I started by teaching him to sit on the pony's back. Then I thought I would teach him to lead a pony. It took me weeks and weeks and an awful lot of patience. I will never forget the day he finally did it. I had persuaded him for hours to get him to bring the pony to me. He was absolutely exhausted, and then suddenly he came, picking his feet up in the air. It was dark - only an oil lamp for light. I hid so that he could not see me, but he led the pony right to me, simply by the sound of my voice. When I realised what we had achieved that night, I took the reins out of his mouth and caught him in my arms and hugged him. I cried like a baby.

I knew then that there were going to be great times ahead of us. All my efforts had not been in vain.

I didn't do this again for a while, but the next time I asked him to fetch the pony, he did it straight away. I will point out later on, how useful this became to me in my work, and what a master he was at doing it. There was something about you, Scott that set you apart from any dog I ever owned. I always said that you thought for yourself. Although I taught many dogs to do many things, you were different. I always felt you had a human brain inside that head of yours.

The biggest regret I have had to live with is parting with you. I thought you were going to a good home to someone who would have loved and cherished you as I had, but unfortunately I never knew how your life ended, only to say that I suspect you were not happy and for that I am so sorry. You deserved so much more than that."

Dad remembered how, not long after he first had Scott, his boss had bought a cow and calf. They were being brought by train to Ynysybwl. The train was due to arrive at 9 o'clock, but didn't arrive until midnight;

while waiting for the delayed train Dad and his boss waited at Dad's sister, Maggie's house in Crawshay Street, not far from the station.

When the cattle eventually arrived they had to walk the cattle three to four miles to Tirgwaidd. After about a mile the cow, probably trying to protect the calf, started attacking Scott, and almost injured Dad and his boss. Dad sent Scott back because it was dangerous and dark and he was afraid he would get harmed. He told him to go home, thinking he would go back to the farm. He didn't see him again that night.

Scott had returned not to the farm, but to Maggie's house. She and her husband were in bed and could hear him barking and jumping up at the latch. Maggie stayed up with him all night, because she was afraid he might jump through a window to get out. When she opened the kitchen door the next morning, off he went making his way to the farm. It amazed both Dad and his boss how Scott had found his way back to Maggie's house. He had never been there before that night.

As the months went by, Dad discovered that he had a really good whistle. He had learnt to whistle very loudly by placing his two fingers in his mouth. As his whistle got louder and clearer, so Scott was able to understand more of his commands.

Every day brought its problems and he found himself searching for a way to solve them. Scott became his 'right arm'. Without him he felt helpless. When he heard someone describing a dog as 'a faithful friend' he felt that Scott was this and even more to him. They became inseparable.

One early difficulty encountered with Scott was his tendency to depend on being able to see Dad in order to follow orders. When he wanted Scott to go right to the top of the mountain to gather sheep (and sometimes this meant several miles away), he would keep looking back to see if Dad was still there. He would have to keep giving him commands to send him on his way. There were times when he would go away so far that he would lose sight of Dad and would start to turn back.

He thought of a way of solving this problem. He would give Scott a command to send him off. He would then hide inside the lamb house from where he could see Scott, but Scott couldn't see him. He would keep whistling and making sure that he went on his way. Eventually it became necessary to only give him one command, and that would take him to wherever the sheep were. It never mattered after that whether he could see Dad or not, he worked simply on Dad's whistles.

Dad was a self-taught trainer. He made many mistakes, but always acknowledged that they were his mistakes and tried to avoid making the same ones again. He always respected his dogs and compared them to human beings. He felt each dog had its own character. Dogs could differ tremendously in temperament; some were bold and afraid of nothing and others were timid and shy. Dad never knew Scott's breeding, but none of that mattered. He was by far the finest dog he had ever owned. Scott's mother must have given birth to forty or fifty pups, all of whom had been drowned at birth. This would have been Scott's fate, had it not been for Maggie. Dad would shudder whenever he thought of it.

The natural instinct of a dog if it is challenged by a sheep is to bite. Dad did not want any of his dogs to bite so he taught Scott to paw the sheep continuously until the sheep would finally give up on the challenge; this worked beautifully. It was quite something to see.

ORPHAN LAMBS

The area Dad had to cover on the hills above the Rhondda Valleys was vast, and was one of the most rugged of terrains to be found in Wales. In his work as a shepherd, he often came across orphan lambs. He would often find an ewe that had difficulty lambing and had died as a result. Next to her would be her lamb, which needed shelter, warmth and milk. Dad would put the lamb in front of him on the horse's back, but he might have been miles away from home. He could not take the lamb home and return to the mountain, because time did not permit this; there might well be another ewe in trouble that he could assist avoiding another death.

It was necessary for him to find some sort of shelter - perhaps just a make-shift pen made from a circle of stones. He would put the orphan lambs in there until his day was over and it was time to return home. He would then have to carry as many lambs as he could manage on the back of the horse to the farm, where he could keep them warm and fed. If by any chance he could not manage them all, he would have to leave perhaps one lamb in the pen on the top of the mountain. He taught Scott to carry a bottle of milk back to the pen and feed the lamb with the bottle. This became an invaluable aid to him and enabled him to carry on with the rest of his work, until such time as he could return to the orphan himself.

One night, Dad had gone to bed after feeding the animals and securing them in the stables for the night. He didn't have a kennel for the dogs; they slept with the horses in the stables. He must have fallen into a very deep sleep, - not unusual as he worked for up to 18 hours a day during the lambing season. Next morning by the breakfast table, his boss and his wife said "Didn't you hear Scott barking last night Tom?" He said "No, what do you mean?" "Well, he kept us awake - he had jumped through a pane of glass in the stable window and was jumping up at the latch on the door and barking like mad - I had to put the whip to him in the end, or we would't have had any sleep at all". Dad was really upset when he heard this. He went out to the stable and found poor old Scott cowering under the stairs leading to the loft. He looked at the broken window, which looked barely big enough for him to have got through. Dad knew instinctively that there must have been good reason for Scott to act like this. He very shortly discovered the reason.

He was given his orders for the day, as usual. On that particular day his orders had been to feed the cows and horses; go across Cae Tir Bedw, across the coal tips, down to Porth and come up the line, bringing all the sheep he found up to the mountain. Away he went. Just a hundred yards from the house, in the brook, he found a dead sheep. It was obvious it had been killed by a dog. On the path to Cae Tir Bedw there was yet another dead sheep. He galloped back to the house to tell his boss. He went off on horseback across the side of the mountain, down towards the Colliery. He asked the Colliery Sergeant, who worked the night shift, if he had heard anything during the night. He said he had heard dogs barking about 1 o'clock in the morning. One of the workmen, who had been riding on the journey up the incline, had seen sheep scattering and two dogs chasing them, one bigger and one smaller dog. The total number of sheep killed that night had been ten.

Dad and his boss stayed up that night. When dogs take to killing, they sometimes follow the same pattern and will travel the same route at the same time. At almost the same time as the workmen had seen them the night before, Dad heard dogs barking. He let Scott out of the stable and away he went. He followed on horseback. He took them to the exact spot where the two dogs, one an Old English sheepdog and a small spaniel were killing a sheep.

Obviously this was why Scott had tried to rouse Dad on the previous night. Scott knew, without any shadow of doubt that it wasn't wise for him to go after the dogs himself, because if anyone had seen him, it would have been assumed that he was with them. Dad's boss felt dreadful when he realised the situation and that he had punished him for doing his job.

Dad was at this time becoming known far and wide for his remarkable talents, and was being asked to give exhibitions all over the country, travelling as far as Birmingham, Bristol etc. He had no transport, and often relied on Mam's brother, Howell, who lived in Ferndale and had a motor bike, to take him wherever he had to go. It was quite common for them to travel miles, Uncle Howell driving, with Dad riding pillion and two dogs and a lamb in between them. Mam (Margaret Jane (nee Thomas)) and Dad met in 1928 when Dad had been working at Blaenllechau Farm. Mam lived in Regent Street, Ferndale, with her parents, David and Sarah Ann Thomas. It was here that they went to live when they got married in 1930. Nancy was born there. The family home was already overcrowded, Mam having three sisters and a brother still living at home, as well as my grandparents. Dad also had Scott and three young dogs. It was necessary for them to look for somewhere else to live, and this presented a problem as far as the dogs were concerned. It meant Dad had to sell some of them. They returned to Ynysybwl, where they lived in front room apartments with various families. They moved three times to different addresses in Ynysybwl, finally living in the front room of Mill House. They remained there for some four years.

During this time, the Ocean Coal Company was buying up farms and was using the mountain to breed sheep. Someone who knew of Dad's expertise with his dogs, suggested to the Colliery Manager in Park and Dare Colliery, that he should be approached, as they were looking for a shepherd. Dad was offered a job and they moved to Cwmparc to live. There was no accommodation provided but he decided to take the job. Once again, the only accommodation they could afford was a front room and a bedroom. This was in Pencai Terrace, where Llinos was born. Dad bought some young dogs from renowned sheep-dog breeders. He trained them, using the knowledge he had gained whilst training Scott. The training of these dogs had to be quite intense as he needed them in order to carry out his role as shepherd in charge of 2,000 ewes on the vast mountains of the Rhondda.

It was whilst they were living at Pencai Terrace that the film 'Sheepdog' was made in 1936. They moved to Ystradfechan Cottages, in 1939, and I was born there in 1940. Both Mam and Dad were very happy living in Treorchy and made some very good friends there. The Second World War had started and times were very hard; Dad's wages were £1 10 shillings a week. For this he had the responsibility of caring for 2,000 sheep.

Being a shepherd on the Rhondda Mountains was certainly no easy job. It was often more hazardous than anyone could ever imagine. The mountains were full of crevices, sometimes quite wide and deep. Nature being what it is, often put Dad in a position where he was faced with problems, which needed his urgent attention. The thought of losing a sheep when it could have been saved, was the worst thing that could happen. Here Scott became invaluable. He seemed so wise, and Dad always felt he had a good friend with him, which could be very reassuring when he was up on the hills, miles from anywhere, and the mists are swirling and the winds howling. It was in conditions such as this that Dad often found himself in.

On one such occasion, he had come across an ewe which was sick. He knew that unless he got her home and treated her, she would die. He had to put her in front of him on the pony's back - she was far too weak to walk. He could not see a thing. The mist was like a blanket and brought an eerie silence with it. Dad said he became completely disorientated. He gave Scott the reins and told him to lead them home. Scott who never failed him did, just that. As they descended the mountain, the mist became less dense and with a great sense of relief, they arrived home.

A few weeks later, torrential rain fell for several days. This had turned a river, which was normally shallow into a deep, fast flowing torrent. Dad could see three sheep stranded on the far side of the river. Their fleeces were saturated and the weight, together with the swirling, gushing, water prevented them from swimming to safety. Scott saw the plight of the sheep and without any warning jumped into the water. He swam across dragging the sheep, one at a time, until they were safely on the riverbank. Dad was so frightened that Scott would drown. It was one of the most remarkable things he had ever witnessed. He felt that this confirmed what he had always thought - that Scott was no ordinary dog.

TRAINER

Dad used Scott to help him when he was training young sheep dogs. He would give him a command to make sure that the sheep stayed in the area that had been designated for training, and if they tried to escape he would bring them back. This enabled Dad to work closely with the young dogs. On one occasion, having finished training for the day, he made his way home with the young dogs following behind. He had completely forgotten about Scott. When he went to feed the dogs and lock them up for the night, he realised that Scott wasn't there. He called and called, and then suddenly remembered that he hadn't given Scott a command to let the sheep go. He went back to where he had left him and there was Scott, still watching, and waiting for his master's command. The sight of him there, almost totally in the dark, brought tears to Dad's eyes. What faithfulness and trust he had in Dad. Dad hoped he would never betray that trust.

SCOTT THINKS FOR HIMSELF

Not far from our home in Treorchy was a busy railway line. Frequently sheep were being killed by trains. One day Dad was on the horse bringing the strays off the road and the railway line, when a lamb refused to move. There was a train coming. Scott sensed that the lamb would bolt, possibly in front of the train. Scott jumped on top of the lamb and literally held it with his two paws on the ground until the train had passed.

On another occasion a stubborn ewe was running straight up the middle of the railway line in front of an oncoming train. The dogs were working as hard as they could to try to move her, but all was in vain. Dad was concerned that the dogs and the sheep would get run over, so he gave the dogs a command to leave the sheep, thinking that its fate was inevitable. As the train drew near, Scott nipped the ewe. She jumped off the line and fell into the river. Scott jumped in after her. Dad didn't realise that the river ran through a tunnel. He could see the ewe and Scott being washed away and thought that both would surely drown. He ran alongside the river, watching with horror. An old mattress had been thrown in the river and had become lodged on the side of the river bank. Scott had somehow managed to push the ewe against the mattress, preventing her from being washed any further down the river. When Dad caught up with them, Scott was holding the ewe by the neck. The ewe and Scott were exhausted and the ewe was too heavy for Scott to pull out. Dad guessed that Scott was as glad to see Dad arrive as he was to see Scott.

LEADING A PONY

During the lambing season, Dad often worked from dawn to dusk. Because of the amount of riding he did on his pony, this meant that the pony had to be shod frequently. Shoeing a horse is a time-consuming activity and it was time that Dad could ill afford. He had another pony which he could use whilst the one was being shod. He wondered how he could find a way to continue working for the period of time it took for the pony to be shod. A way of getting the pony back to the farm without Dad returning would have to be found.

He took the pony to the Blacksmith and asked him if it would be alright if he left him there with Scott. Dad said that when the blacksmith had finished shoeing the pony, Scott would bring him back home if he put the reins in Scott's mouth. The Blacksmith looked at Dad as if he was deranged. Dad assured him that there would be no problem - all he had to do was put the reins in Scott's mouth and let him go. This became a regular occurrence. People became used to seeing Scott leading the pony up the main road.

Scott holding 'Christy' outside Burgess, Chemist, The Strand, Ferndale

Dad never taught Scott anything that wasn't going to be useful to him. He taught him to ride 'pillion' behind him on the horses back, putting his paws around his neck to hold on. To some people, this would appear to be sheer showmanship, but by Scott standing on the pony's back, he was able to see much further ahead of him. The mountain was made up of very rough tufts of grass, and when Scott was at ground level, he could not see very far ahead. One occasion when this proved to be particularly valuable was when they were out shepherding. Scott was standing up behind Dad. He began to paw him and bark. Dad had learnt never to ignore these signs. He could hear and see nothing of significance, but Scott persisted. Dad let Scott get off the pony and he ran ahead. Guide, one of his other dogs, was with them. Dad sent one dog off to the right and one to the left. When they reached the top of the hill, Dad could see a dog in the process of killing a sheep. Between the three of them, they managed to catch the killer.

'WELSH WONDER SHEPHERD OF THE RHONDDA'

One morning Dad and Scott had been out very early. They were bringing an ewe and twins home on the back of the pony. Scott was leading the pony because Dad could not hold on to the sheep and the reins at the same time. He was stopped by a man as they neared the colliery. He said he had been sent to fetch him - Dad was wanted in the Colliery Office. When he got there, the Secretary asked him what had Scott been doing going across the mountain the day before. He said he had been watching him through the binoculars and saw Scott leading the pony. He could not see Dad. Dad said that he had given him the reins and told him to take the pony home.

At that time, the Ocean Coal Company, Dad's employer, published a monthly magazine. Each Colliery submitted items of local news. The secretary said he was going to write an article about Scott. He asked Dad whether he had any other things to write about. Dad told him about the dogs feeding lambs with a bottle etc. What he didn't know at the time was that the secretary was also a reporter for the local newspaper. He was so excited hearing Dad's account of Scott's skill that he arranged for a reporter from Cardiff to come up the following day.

Amongst the skills the reporter witnessed was that of the dogs feeding lambs. The year had been a bad one for sheep. Several of the ewes had a form of mastitis - a painful condition of the teat. They had not let their lambs suckle. Consequently there was an unusually high number of lambs being bottle fed. There were fourteen in all and this meant Dad could be tied up for hours feeding them all - time which he could ill afford. Dad had three dogs and they were all able to feed lambs with a bottle. He gave them each a bottle and when they had fed one lamb, they would go on to feed the next.

The reporter was amazed and was so excited at what he had witnessed that he advertised his article on notice boards and placards bearing the words 'Welsh Wonder Shepherd of the Rhondda.' Suddenly, Scott and Dad had become famous. He was being contacted by people from all over the country, asking him to give exhibitions. At the same time he was competing in Sheep Dog trials.

'KEN'

At Aberystwyth, in the same year, Dad was competing in the National Sheep Dog Trial. He was approached by a friend who said that his brother had a dog that would suit him. He said that his brother had trained the dog and given him to a friend, but that he could not get him to work. After the trial had finished, Dad asked whether he could put the dog around the sheep used for the trial. He asked for the command that the dog knew. He gave the command and the dog went out without any problem at all. Dad thought he was very graceful and really liked him. Dad was a little bit wary of why his friend was selling such a good dog, and asked him whether there was anything wrong with him. He was assured that the dog, Ken, was perfectly fit and healthy. The deal was done. Dad gave him a few pounds and one of his young dogs in payment.

When he arrived home, he kept him in for a few days to acclimatise to his surroundings. He took him out to a small field which he used to train his dogs. The dog heard the sheep. Dad let him go and he ran straight into a wall. He knew then that Ken was blind. He took him to a vet, Jim Brown. He tested his eyes and said "His candles have gone out".

Dad felt there was something lovely about the dog's nature. He had a good pedigree - his mother being an International Sheepdog Trial winner. Dad couldn't part with him. He trained him to feed a lamb, carry a dead lamb, lead a pony and competed with him in a trial on Gellionen Farm, gaining a second prize. However, in practical terms, shepherding was impossible for a dog without sight. He could work on the mountain, but because Dad had to go down to the village every day to bring the stray sheep back home, Ken would bump into obstacles such as refuse bins which had been put out on the streets.

Dad felt it was unkind to the dog to continue trying to work him as a sheepdog. Dad's brother, Stan, lived with his mother in Ynysybwl and would get offal from the slaughterhouse, boil it and bring it to Tirgwaidd every week for Dad to feed the dogs. He agreed to take Ken.

The first Sunday after Ken had been left with Stan, Dad was cleaning out the stable early in the morning. He happened to look down the road, which came down from the mountain. He could see Ken with his nose to the ground like a hound. Dad ran into the stable and hid behind the door.

Ken came into the stable where Dad was hiding. Ken was jumping and barking and Dad felt it was as if he talking to him in his way. He thought that Stan would be coming up behind him, but there was no sign of him. Ken would not leave Dad's side, and it was as if he was saying "I have found you, and I'm never going to leave you again."

Later that day Stan arrived. He said he had been looking everywhere for Ken. Sadly, this was to be Ken's last walk over the mountain. A few days later he died. Dad was convinced that he had died of a broken heart. He used to say that dogs were like humans, they had the same feelings. They could be happy and they could be sad. He often said he wondered who came first, dog or man!

'Ken' leading a pony

THE PARTING OF THE WAYS

The hardest thing Dad ever had to do was to part with Scott. Many people over the years asked him what had happened to him. He never told anyone, because he couldn't bear to face up to what he had done. He had kept this to himself all his life.

It was 1938. Nancy, Dad's 'mother' was having a bad time. Her husband was a cruel man, who used to beat her. She wanted a legal separation from him (which was necessary before she could apply for a divorce). The solicitor's fee for applying for the separation was five pounds. She did not know who she could borrow the money off. She visited Dad to ask him. Dad had no money, but because out of loyalty to his mother, he felt he had to find the money from somewhere.

The only way he could raise this money was to sell one of his dogs. Scott was now 15 years old. Dad had several other young dogs. The Ocean Coal Company had amalgamated with another company and they were giving up all the farms that were in their ownership. The sheep were being sold and Dad knew that his job was coming to an end and he would be made redundant.

He knew that the most valuable dog would be Scott. He met a Police Sergeant who asked him if he had an old dog that he would sell. The intention was to give the dog to his father, who had a small-holding in North Wales. He wanted a dog that he could trust. Dad said that he would sell him the grandest dog a man could ever own - on condition that if he didn't suit him, he would send him back. He also told him that if he died, he would like his body sent back so that he could be buried at home. He would pay all the expenses.

The following passage is taken from Dad's manuscript, and is presented exactly as he wrote it:

> "I wish I had never seen that man, because when I saw him he as good as said that I had sent him a useless dog. He was no good. I told him only about 200 yards from where he was standing at the time I had given an exhibition with him. There was hardly a park throughout South Wales that he hadn't given a

display in. I asked him what had happened to Scott. He did not satisfy me with an answer. I shall never forget the morning I took him to the station to book him on the train. I could not stop to see him going. I asked the Porter to be careful with him when putting him on the train. It is an awful thing to say, I cried all the way home and still cry when I talk about him, I can't help it. I had been trying to think what had happened to him. Had he shot him or did he try to find his way back. I have been wondering ever since. I can quite understand why he would not work for his father. I was having trouble to understand the North Welsh accent myself and probably Scott wouldn't have understood him either. Another thing, the dog had never been from me. He was lost. What must have he been feeling? He couldn't talk, but God as I am writing this, I can picture his face looking around for me. What would have been his reaction if he had seen me, if the man had done what I had asked him and sent him back if he didn't like him not condemn the greatest dog that ever lived. He was so gentle, and yet so brave and tackled any dog that was worrying sheep.''

Dad felt as if he had betrayed Scott and couldn't bear to think of what the dog had felt when Dad parted with him. Until the end of his days, Dad regretted his decision to sell Scott, but he did what he thought was the right thing to do at the time.

CHAPTER 3

SHEEPDOG TRIALS

Over many years Dad had a very successful record whilst competing in Sheep Dog Trials all over the country. During the Trial Season, he competed almost every weekend, often travelling to two or three trials a day. It is difficult to even hazard a guess at how many trials he competed in over his years, but the first one we have a record of was in 1929 and the last one was in the 1970's, so it was over some 40 years.

Here are just a few of the photographs (some of which have survived 80 years and more).

Dad and his pal Wyndham Harries at Llandrindod Wells Sheep Dog Trial in 1929, looking very happy!!!!!

A lovely group of Sheepdogs waiting their turn to take part in the Sheep Dog Trials again in Llandrindod Wells.

Dad with Gypsy at one of the local trials

Gypsy with various cups

Guide (son of Henderson's Guide)   He won this cup three times out of four. This was an "outright" cup, which meant that once it had been won three times by the same person, that person could keep it. It is a magnificent cup, and is still in the family today, along with many of the others Dad won.

Dad training his dogs at Tyle'r Fedw. This dog's name was Tam, bought from a John Purdie, who was from Scotland. Tam was a master at penning sheep and Dad described him as being "As firm as a rock". Dad bought many pups from him including Queen who Dad nicknamed "The Artist" because she had such style about her. Here the two of them, Queen and Tam, are pictured penning the sheep in the pen Dad used for training his dogs.

Mr. T. Jones, of Cwmparc, Treorchy
Inner of the Novice Class with "Chip."

Dad with a dog called "Chip", after they had won a Novice Class at a sheep dog trial. A Novice Class was a Class where only dogs who had never won an Open Class could compete. This was a chance for young dogs to compete against other novice dogs.

WONDER SHEPHER

Dad competing at Birmingham in 1931. The dogs were Scott, Chip and Guide.

Sweep with the Frank Ann Cup, which he won at Aberaman. Sweep was the son of 'Dickson's Hemp'.

Dogs and masters equally intently watching a competition at
the Welsh national trials at Margam. Or are they watching
Dai Lossin being penned on the other side of this page?

Dad with some of his sheepdog friends waiting for their turn.at the Welsh
National Sheep Dog Trials at Margam, Port Talbot,

Dad also competed in many other years at the National Sheep Dog Trials.
For example, we know he competed at the Welsh National Trials at
Dogellau in 1962. In another year at Prestatyn, he tied for 2nd and 3rd
place in the Shepherds' National Cup, with Guide scoring 86 points out of
a possible 120. He also came fourth in the same competition with Chip,
who scored 82 points.   He won the class for 'Oustanding Style' with
Guide.   In the Farmers' Class he won the prize for the best conditioned
dog, Chip.

CHAPTER 4

THE SHEPHERD

One thing Dad had learnt was that no shepherd should take the mountains for granted. Because of the terrain, and the danger of crevices which were sometimes not visible shepherds often relied on their ponies, who somehow could sense danger. The pony would often leap to one side or another, and refuse to go on.

Dad had often heard the pitiful bleat of a lamb or lambs that had fallen down one of the crevices. He had heard their cries getting weaker and weaker every time he passed, but had been unable to locate them. On one occasion, however, he was lucky. There were about six shepherds out, gathering sheep for a neighbour in readiness for shearing. Each shepherd had his own 'patch' to cover. They gathered in a huge circle. Their first job was to gather the sheep off the streets. As they were approaching the hills, the mist came down. Mist has an odd way of deadening sounds. They could hear almost nothing - not even the whistles of the other shepherds. They became completely disorientated and had no idea where they were. Although they were very familiar with the territory, they had no sense of direction because they couldn't see anything. Dad waited for the mist to clear. His dogs wandered off a little way. They came back and were whining and obviously trying to alert Dad that there was something wrong. He followed them. There was a crevice 8 - 10 feet wide and about 10 feet deep. A lamb could be seen on a ledge. Dad couldn't go down without a rope. In order to mark the spot, he put his shepherd's crook into the ground, so that as soon as the mist cleared he could go, get help and get the lamb up. The mountain, the 'Bwllfa', in Ton Pentre, was the worst he had ever seen for crevices. On most mountains, the crevices ran along the mountain, but there was no pattern to the crevices here and they seemed to be everywhere, running in all different directions.

He found two of the shepherds, Tom and Llew Morgan, whose sheep they were helping to gather. They fetched a rope. When they arrived back at the crevice there was no sign of the lamb. Dad was certain where it had been because his crook was marking the spot. There was a small crack in the ground. He put his ear to it and could hear the lamb bleating, but it sounded a long way off. He realised that the lamb must have tried to get to the surface and had fallen further down. A longer rope was obtained and they borrowed a lamp from the Colliery. Dad tied a rope around his waist and Llew and Tom lowered him down. Llew told Dad not to risk his life for a lamb, but Dad couldn't bear to hear the lamb bleating without at least attempting a rescue. Little did he know what was in front of him. There was not one, but three lambs there. The crevice was barely wide enough for Dad to descend. He descended 79 feet in all, a frightening experience, particularly when one considers that he was in darkness for much of the time and could hear nothing apart from cracking noises coming from the ground and the sound of stones falling.

The R.S.P.C.A. came to hear of the rescue and Dad was awarded the Silver Medal for Humanity.

FAITHFULNESS

One thing that never ceased to amaze Dad was the faithfulness of his dogs. Whilst riding along Graig Fawr in Cwmparc, he noticed a sheep up on a ledge. He thought he could persuade her to turn back. He estimated the cliff to be about 300 feet high. Dad left one of the dogs holding the pony on the top of the cliff and started to descend. He had a young bitch with him, who was only partly trained. He didn't think that she would have followed him. He started his way down, his only anchor points being clumps of heather onto which he could cling. He had descended about 40 feet, when he could see the little bitch trying to follow him. Soon afterwards he could see her tumbling down, hitting the rocks as she fell. He clung to the rock face, afraid to look down to the bottom. He was there for hours. The ledge was too narrow. He felt absolutely stuck and that he could neither advance nor return. He said that only by the grace of God did he make his way to the bottom where the poor little dog had landed. He thought she was dead. He put his two hands under her, trying not to hurt her any more. She gave a little whimper. He had to leave her in a pen on the top of the mountain whilst he took some sheep about a mile down to the farm. As soon as he had taken them, he returned, but the dog was not there. He hunted everywhere. He searched until it became too dark, but she was nowhere to be seen. He got up early the next morning and went out to the stable to fetch a pony to go and look for her. There the dog was found. She had dragged herself down to the gate of the yard and died.

Thinking about it later, he said he wished he had thought more about what he had done that day. It was certainly a hard lesson to learn. He said he knew what the saying 'faithful unto death' really meant. The little bitch didn't want him to go without her, so she followed him to her death and then, when he left her she couldn't bear that either, and used what was the last breath she had to go home to him. He regretted so much leaving her there - but life is full of 'if only' isn't it?

Whenever young shepherds asked him for advice, Dad told them not to take unnecessary risks. He advised them to always consider the circumstances before deciding whether it is safe for a dog to accompany them. If a shepherd has a good dog, the dog puts his entire trust in him. The shepherd must never betray that trust and ask the impossible of the dog. He emphasised that the dog is the best friend a shepherd will ever have.

Nothing gave Dad more of a thrill than, during the lambing season, seeing the first little white spot on the mountain. A new life had been created, and he was now completely responsible for its care.

There were happy times and there were sad times. One day, he witnessed an ewe standing by the side of her offspring. When he got close, he could see the poor little thing struggling to get up. There was blood coming out of her mouth. He picked her up. A magpie had pecked out the tongue right to the back of its throat. The bird was sitting on a wall nearby and it was as if the poor mother was trying to tell him. The only merciful thing Dad could do for that lamb was to end its life and hope to find another lamb for the ewe to foster.

Crows were another menace to a shepherd. Dad recalled how he came across an ewe lambing. He was quite far away and could see two crows, one on the ground and one on a tree. He galloped over as fast as he could, but he was too late. The ewe was too weak; the crows had pecked her eyes out before the lamb was fully delivered. Dad completed the delivery of the lamb but it was dead. He carried the ewe back to the barn, where she stayed for a fortnight. She was coming along well, but someone left the door open one day and she had gone. Dad knew exactly where she would go. He jumped on the pony to look for her. Like a good mother she had gone to look for her child. She was ill and he had no alternative but to put her to sleep. He buried her where he knew she wanted to be - where she had given birth to her lamb.

These are just some insights into the work of a good shepherd. The life of a shepherd is so different from any other. Every lamb and every ewe is the shepherd's responsibility. Few shepherds do the job for monetary gain; they do it because it is what matters to them.

RHONDDA SHEPHERD'S GALLANT RESCUE

'From the lonely heather clad summit of the Bwllfa Mountain that lies mid-way between Clydach Vale and Ton Pentre, and where crevices abound – the depths of which man has not yet solved, and where the silence is only broken by the curlew's whistle and the Bittern's call intermingled with the bleating of sheep, comes the thrilling story of a shepherd's successful rescue of three lambs who had fallen into one of these many crevices and who but for the shepherd and his ever watchful dogs, would undoubtedly have perished from hunger in their entombment. The hero of this lonely mountain drama was Mr Tom Jones, Treorchy – The Welsh Wonder Shepherd, in the employ of the Ocean Coal Company Ltd. Interviewed by our Cwmparc Representative, Mr Jones being of a rather retiring disposition, seemed at first a little reluctant in giving a narration of his experience, regarding it merely part of his daily routine. However, when pressed, he consented.

It has been the age long custom in the Valley of local shepherds, rendering assistance to each other, when gathering their flocks for washing, shearing and the dipping process. Each shepherd and his dogs, go in different directions, and drive the sheep to a final given point. Mr Jones with his dogs Chip, Bob and Guide on Tuesday of last week, were assisting in the gathering of the flock owned by Mr. T. Morgan of the Maindy Farm. Having taken a given direction, and awaiting to be rejoined by his co-gatherers, Mr Jones's attention was drawn in the direction of his dogs, peering over a crevice, and at intervals looked back at him, wagging their tails as if in doggy language, required his immediate presence. Going over, Mr Jones discovered a lamb on a ledge 20 to 30 feet down. Whilst preparing to make a descent, a heavy mist arose over the scene, making it impossible to be visible 20 yards away. Mr. Jones found it impossible to make a descent, without the assistance of a rope, inasmuch as stones were continually giving way above and beneath him. Soon his keen sense of hearing picked up the piteous cry of another lamb, lower down in the darkness of the crevice. The mist came down heavier, and it was impossible to render any aid to the two little prisoners below. Mr Jones for a mark stuck his staff in the ground and made his way back to the starting point. He related what he had seen and it was decided to make an attempt at down next day. True to their promise the shepherds, with ropes and a miner's lamp borrowed from a colliery made their way at daybreak, to relieve the little prisoners. Upon reaching the crevice and peering down, it was discovered that the lamb first seen by Mr Jones was not on the ledge, neither could any bleating be heard. Mr Jones, however, was unsatisfied, and made up his mind to descent, if only to find the dead bodies. The lamb must have dropped into the inky depth below the ledge, as it was impossible for it to have reached the surface unaided. With a rope tied around his waist, Mr Jones was lowered on to the crevice, and then lowered down a further 70 feet. Here he discovered a cleft with just sufficient room for him to walk along sideways for a distance between 10 to 15 feet. Here came a further drop. Tying his lamp on a rope, he lowered it into the hole, and was astonished to find three moving objects. A further descent found him standing before three lambs, whilst far above his head gleamed light from a hole, where undoubtedly the last two had fallen through. How long they had been there cannot be told, since many hours had even passed when Mr. Jones discovered the first lamb. None of the three little prisoners offered resistance inasmuch as one had sustained a minor injury to his back and the other two minor leg injuries. Carefully securing a rope around each, Mr Jones gave the signal for those above to wind up very slow, whilst he guided their journey to freedom, one at a time when all the time stones and debris continually became loosened, through being rubbed against. With the lambs safe above ground, Mr Jones slowly was pulled up, and when surface was reached he heaved a sigh of real thankfulness for having come up safe. Little to mention that he was warmly congratulated by his anxious co-shepherds, since a slip of the foot would have meant sure death.'

(A report from a local newspaper, c1931)

The

Royal Society for the Prevention of Cruelty to Animals

Under Her Majesty the King

●

This is to Certify that the
Silver Medal of the Society
has been awarded to Mr T. Jones
for his courage and humanity
in rescuing some lambs from a
crevice 70 feet deep at Tworehy,
Naws, on July 6th 1939.

Dated this 27th day of July 1939

Chairman

Chief
Secretary

Founded
1824

SOME OTHER REMINISCENCES OF SHEPHERDING

Dad talked of many different incidents that he had witnessed out on the mountain while shepherding. One of these is quite fascinating to read. Whilst out on the mountain one morning, he saw a sheep that had just lambed. As he glanced across, he saw a fox coming towards the sheep. There was a wall not far away, so Dad hid behind it and when the fox spotted the lamb, Dad said to himself "He must be thinking here's my dinner", but the ewe didn't take her eyes off him. Dad said, like humans, not all mothers are good mothers. Some don't care what happens to the children, and this is the same for animals. This sheep however was different. She watched his every move and kept her lamb behind her. The fox tried to make her think that he was not interested in the lamb, and he went to roll and slide around, but all the time, getting closer and closer. The fox got to his feet, as if he was fed up of pretending, and he made a dive for the lamb, but the ewe hit him over and still she managed to keep her lamb behind her. The fox tried and tried again. The ewe made a horrible bleating sound, which must have frightened him; the fox called it a day and off he trotted over the mountain to his lair, to where he had probably carried many lambs. It was a wonderful event to have witnessed.

During the lambing season, the shepherd has to be out from daylight to dusk. In his hand-written notes, Dad asked the question of the reader "Have you ever felt numb with cold?" Dad described how several times he has had this experience. He said he had seen lambs frozen to the ground, horses with icicles hanging from their nostrils and often his own eyes feeling as if they were frozen together and having to force them open.

Often when there was a sheep lambing and having difficulty, he felt there was a guiding hand leading him somehow to where she was. He said that after years of travelling the mountain, he knew where to go to get the best vantage points, so that he could see large areas around him. He would see paths which had been made by him through travelling regularly, but for some reason, he would be made on occasions to alter his course. He said he didn't know why, but he just knew that something was telling him that a sheep needed help. He said that had happened on several occasions, and he would find a sheep, which was unable to lamb and was in a poor shape. It could be freezing, or snowing, or raining or a blizzard. He would examine the sheep and try to find out whether the lamb was alive or dead. Sometimes he could not feel the lamb's head or feet and could not make out which way it was laying in the womb. He said he would ask God for help. He would try to cause as little pain as he could for the ewe and at last he would find out the position in which the lamb was lying and then deliver the lamb safely. Through the difficult birth, the lamb would often be lifeless, but after rubbing it to try to warm it, the lamb would suddenly shake its head and perhaps bleat. He would then put it in front of his mother who would start to lick the lamb and the ewe would stand and make a fuss of it. Dad would get a thrill every time this happened and knew that it was safe for him to carry on his journey.

Dad often talked about one of the shepherds, who was a dear friend of his boss. His name was Harry Williams or 'Harry Ffaldau' as he was called, Ffaldau being the name of the farm where he lived. Dad said "Now without a word of a lie, he had a voice you could hear from a mile away". Harry had three dogs- Merry, Bonnie and Llank. He used Llank for coursing on banking, to keep behind the sheep to send them on the mountain and off the streets. Dad said that when they were coming up the valleys, it was the loveliest sound a young shepherd could ever hear. He would be thrilled to see the lambs coming in a drove and the dogs barking, everyone so busy and oblivious to anything that was going on around them. He could remember Harry shouting on top of his voice at Llank, and boy – could he shout! Those were the days before lorries. It was nature in the raw.

However difficult times could be Dad loved his work. Seeing the mountain in all its glory, beauty and ruggedness that had been there forever always filled him with wonder. It saddened him that future generations would never know what that was like, when the fields and mountains all had their own names, just as streets and rivers have now.

CHAPTER 5

'SHEEPDOG'

The year was 1936. Scott's fame was spreading all over the country. Dad was giving exhibitions in places such as Birmingham, Chelsea and all parts of South Wales. One day he had a telephone call from a gentleman in London. He said he had heard about the wonderful things Dad was doing with his dogs and ponies and was interested in making a film. He asked if he could come to see him. Films were a relatively new invention, and Dad couldn't believe that someone wanted him, Tommy Jones, a shepherd in the Rhondda, to make a film.

Scott was now getting too old to do the job as well as he used to, so Dad had trained some young dogs to do the same things as Scott had done. He had bought a pup and by this time he was very accomplished in feedings the lambs, leading the pony, etc. He was a pretty dog, not at all like Scott. He was almost totally white, with two black ears and a black patch on his back.

A meeting was arranged. John Alderson said that he wanted to make a film of the day in the life of a shepherd. He wanted to incorporate as much of the shepherd's life as he could and as the lambing season is one of the most busy times, it was arranged to start filming when the lambing season would begin. Dad had almost 2000 sheep in his care and naturally the lambing season was the busiest of all for him. Technology was at a very early stage, and this meant that the filming needed to take place when the daylight was fairly good. This proved to be very difficult. The late winter and early spring days were still short. In order to accommodate the requirements of the film director, Dad would get up before day break to go around the sheep, making sure that there was no ewe having difficulty in giving birth. The weather was poor and it seemed to rain constantly. Dad would stay out on the mountain if the day was dark, when he knew that filming would be impossible. If the weather was brighter, he would gallop back from wherever he was working to the site where the filming was taking place.

The film took about three months to make. During this time, the weather had been harsh; there had been a heavy fall of snow and a lot of heavy rain. This inevitably put even more pressure on Dad, but he made it clear from the very start that the filming had to fit in around his work and the weather; his sheep had to come first.

Dad with his father-in-law, David Thomas

At the first meeting between Dad and John Alderson, they had discussed at length the job of the shepherd and his dogs. Dad had told him what he had been able to teach the dogs, and in particular he was able to tell John Anderson of the remarkable abilities of Scott. Some of the skills earlier became the basis of many of the film's individual scenes.

The first frames of the film showed Dad going out early in the morning to do his day's shepherding. These first images were followed by scenes that aimed to show many of the problems which faced a shepherd every day of his working life.

One scene demonstrated an occasion when Scott had heard a killer dog at work and jumped out of the window to alert Dad. Dad was in bed but Scott was barking and jumping up at the latch of the door until he woke his master. The scene showed Dad getting up, saddling the pony and telling Scott to lead the way. Scott ran in front of him and took him to the place where there was an Alsatian killing a sheep. This was some two miles away from the farm, but Scott had heard the frantic barking of the dog and knew that something was terribly wrong. Dad had two other dogs with him; Guide and Chip. The three dogs separated, one to the right, one to the left and the other in the middle. The killer was cornered and Dad, who had taken his shotgun with him, shot the Alsatian. This was quite a poignant scene in the film. Dad took the collar off the dog's neck. It had the name of the owner on it. It was someone that Dad knew. The narrator said "Tom, with the compassion of a true dog-lover, knew that there was no alternative but to destroy the killer-dog, even though it be the pet of a colleague or friend". The film went on to show the results of the dog's destruction - counting the bodies of ewes and also new born lambs with their throats ripped out.

The next scene was to show an ewe and lamb, which had got lodged on a ledge after stampeding over a quarry. It showed Dad descending to the ledge and bringing both the lamb and ewe up the quarry face to safety. To do this he was shown tying the ewe and lamb's legs so that he could lift them up bodily. One amazing scene was that which showed Dad finding a dead ewe with her recently born lamb trying to suckle her. He took the lamb to a makeshift pen of stone walling on the top of the mountain. He told Scott to remember where the lamb was. He carried on for the rest of the day and when he returned back to the farm in the evening, he filled a bottle with milk, gave it to Scott, who carried it in his mouth and told him to go and feed the little orphan. The film crew followed Scott as he went on his way eventually finding the pen. He jumped over the stone wall, fed the lamb and returned home. The members of the film crew were absolutely amazed at what they had witnessed. Nothing had been rehearsed. The event had occurred and they had filmed it as it was.

Another scene, filmed on the following day, showed how much Dad relied on Scott to help him in his work. It showed Scott holding the pony with the reins in his mouth whilst Dad was attending to a sick ewe. The ground was inaccessible for the horse. Dad gave Scott a command and he was able to lead the pony around the difficult area, and brought him right to where Dad was. This enabled Dad to put the sheep on the saddle in front of him and with Scott riding 'pillion' standing on the back of the horse, behind the saddle, with his two paws around Dad's neck, they rode home.

In another scene an ewe that had just lambed was frantically trying to revive her dead offspring. Dad caught a little lamb with his shepherd's crook. The lamb was one of twins and the mother had a poor supply of milk. The scene showed him skinning the dead lamb, the skin resembling an overcoat, with the tail intact and the legs like a pair of trousers. He put the skin on top of the twin lamb and placed her with the mother of the dead lamb. She sniffed it for quite a while before finally accepting that it was her lamb and allowing it to suckle. Once the ewe's milk had been drunk, the scent of the ewe passed through the lamb and it was fostered without any problem at all.

PREMIERE AT ODEON CINEMA, LEICESTER SQUARE

The film, 'Sheep Dog', was made by British Screen Services and had its premiere at the Odeon Cinema, Leicester Square, London, in 1939. A member of the royal family was present at its first showing. It was acclaimed as the finest nature film ever made. It was shown all over the world and was selected from hundreds of nature films to be shown in the New York World Fair.

Over the years, letters from all parts of the world arrived especially from Welsh people living in Australia and New Zealand who had seen the film in their local cinemas. A lady who used to call at the house to collect insurance premiums said that she had had a letter from her husband who had been wounded in the 1939-1945 war. He was in hospital in Tubrook. The film had been shown to the patients. Seeing the film and the mountains of his home in Wales had made him feel homesick and lonely. He had cried because he had often watched Dad training the dogs when he lived in Treorchy.

Years after making the film, Dad received a letter from Wellington, New Zealand. The envelope was addressed 'Tom Jones, Welsh Wonder Shepherd, Treorchy'; miraculously it found him. It was from a young soldier stationed in New Zealand. He had gone to the cinema one night and the film 'Sheep Dog' had been shown. He had been born and raised in Treorchy and had been overcome when he recognised the mountains of Treorchy where the film had been made; he felt he had to write to someone to say that he had seen it.

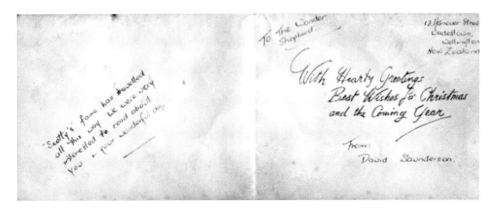

Unfortunately, Dad had been ill-advised when discussions about how much he was to receive from the making of the film took place. Being naive and of a trusting nature, he did not take advice from a solicitor or agent, but made his own deal with John Alderson.

He actually received the total sum of £31 (approximate value in 2011 = £1150). Originally he was sent a cheque for just £16 - £2 10 shillings for the use of the pony; 30 shillings for Scott; £2 10 shillings for Howell (Dad's brother in law who had helped him during the making of the film) and £10 for himself. Despite an appeal to the Film Company he was sent a further cheque for just £15. This arrived with a letter from John Alderson:

> "I am sure you will agree that the total you have received now represents a very good return for your cooperation - it is more actually than we should pay a regular film artiste for what we call a 'short' film, but I am not forgetting that you and your dogs, and the way you did your stuff, has made the film go much better than I expected"…."In the meantime, you will be interested to hear that "Sheep Dog" of all British Nature Films, has been selected to appear at the New York World's Fair. That is a feather in both our caps, my friend."

Some of the correspondence, advertising material and newspaper reports are shown in the pages that follow.

... I have forwarded your letter to the proprietors of the film.

ELMBRIDGE 3270

21. VICTORIA AVENUE.
SURBITON.
SURREY.

6th March 1939.

Dear Tom,

If you have anything to write to me about, don't you think it would be better to do it yourself instead of getting a third party to type a letter which obviously is not you. You write a very good letter & when I'm talking to a man I like to talk to him — & not to a mouthpiece.

However, that is rather beside the point — which is your remark about "percentage payments". First of all, I did not promise you anything. As I was only an employee in the matter, I had no authority to do so. But I believe I did say that, if the film were a success, I would

52

2.

certainly endeavour to get you a
further payment. Well, I have done
so & if the film is a financial
success — as I now believe it will
be — it will not be my fault if you
don't get something further.

But don't expect much. The
film cost quite a bit of money to make
— none of which has come back yet —
& the revenue from "short" films is
ridiculously & unfairly small. Ask
your friend Mr. Watkins. Incidentally,
I myself have not yet received a penny
for my services — & I wrote & produced
the film!

I thought you would be pleased
to hear of the good report of the film from
the point of view of personal achievement.
From your remarks about Cardiff, you
will undoubtedly get some good
publicity. Yours sincerely,

Mrs. E. Wdesign.

53

If you wish to show this letter to Mr Thomas
I have no objection.

21, VICTORIA AVENUE.
SURBITON.
SURREY.

27th March 1939.

Dear Tom –

I'm sorry to have been so
long answering your letter but have
been chasing up some spare leaflets
(enclosed), & also trying to get in touch
with Mr Searle about those "still"
photos. Unfortunately, he says he
can't find the negatives, so we are
both unfortunate, as the only ones I
have myself are very rough amateur
prints.

I was not sore with you,
old man, only a trifle hurt, but your
letter explained the whole circumstances
& I quite understand. Actually, it
was very decent of Mr Thomas to
interfere in what he considered were

I think I explained before that the majority of cinemas pay a fixed price for these short films, however good they may be, and a mighty small price it is, too. Of course, a good film will book to more cinemas and fortunately for all of us, they regard 'Sheep Dog' as a good one — though at one time I was afraid it would't make enough to pay for its cost.

However, the public seem to like my films on animals, & I hope one day to think up another story to make around you & your dogs — if you would care to help me. Perhaps I shall then be able to finance it myself, & neither of us will have to wait for our money.

I am sending you a cheque as I don't like to send notes with this I.R.A. business going on. No doubt Mr Thomas will cash it for you.

With kind regards to you all.

Yours sincerely John C. Anderson

BRITIS UTILITY FILMS LIMITED

Producers and Distributors of Educational, Advertising and Industrial Films

Directors:
...

10, REGENT SQUARE
LONDON :: W.C.I

Telephone ...

15th May 1938.

Dear Von,

I was very glad to have your letter this morning – my first day at the office since I returned from Wales. Mr. Searle and I had an excellent trip back but I brought a beautiful cold with me, a real snorter which laid me low for a few days. Since that, I have been up at the laboratories, cutting and editing the film.

I'm dreadfully sorry about the delay in sending the cash and ought to be ashamed of myself for not realising that it might make things awkward for you. As I told you, however, it was not a B.U.F. production and, when I returned, the actual sponsor was away in Hungary and only recently got back. Still, had I thought of it, I could at least have sent you enough on account to let you square your indebtedness re the pony and Scott.

After all your kindness to Searle and myself, you must have thought me infernally rude not even to write and let you know we had arrived safely. I hated doing so, however, until I could send you the funds and, working on the film, the time simply slipped away. It doesn't seem possible it's a fortnight since we left Treorchy.

I am now enclosing Sixteen Pounds – Pony £2:10:0, Scott 30/-, Howell £2:10:0 (if you think that O.K.) and £10: 0:0 for yourself. I thought you'd prefer notes to a cheque as you don't want everybody in Treorchy to know your business. Perhaps you'll let me have the enclosed form of receipt for my records.

I hope the film is going to turn out allright, although I've a lot of work to do on it yet. Anyhow, it will at least provide a number of new pictures for your collection. As soon as I have a moment, I'll make some enlargements and send them on.

I shall always cherish very happy memories of my trip to Wales – despite the cussedness of the weather – and, if I do get a chance of returning, you bet I'll make a bee-line for Pencai Terrace.

"SHEEP DOG"

Written and Produced by
JOHN ALDERSON

Narrated by
NEAL ARDEN

IF you forsake the deep valley and follow the river towards its source high up in the barren Welsh mountains, you may happen across a lonely, solitary white cottage nestling amongst the foothills.

It is here that our picture opens - soon to carry you away with the exhilarating glory of sweeping landscape and mountain air.

It is in this lovely setting, also, that we introduce you to Tom Jones, his sheep, and his beloved dogs. They call Tom the "Wonder Shepherd" of the Welsh hills.

You shall see just how man and dog tend their wide scattered flock - how, in all weathers, together they rule over the kingdom of the Sheep - a vast realm of undulating country, of snowclad heights, of rough and dangerous slopes.

You shall witness little episodes of tragedy - and how a bereaved mother-sheep is deceived into accepting a substitute for her dead offspring.

Above all, our picture reveals vividly how the minds of Man and Dog uncannily co-operate in the task of preserving the wellbeing of their lowly subjects in their vast mountain solitude.

(LENGTH : 1380 ft. - CERTIFICATE U.)

A PICTURE THAT WILL APPEAL TO ALL ANIMAL LOVERS.

A BRITISH QUOTA PICTURE

BRITISH SCREEN SERVICE

54-58, WARDOUR STREET, LONDON, W.1.

Telephone Gerrard 4343-4-5

Life slowly returns to the frail body of the lamb as Tom Jones warms it before the fire in his cottage, his tenderness being symbolic of his age-old craft. Even more enthralling than the picture of a shepherd working his dogs on the hillside is the sight of such a man warming an orphaned lamb at his fireside

But there are other lambs to be tended, ones to be rescued from precipitous ledges where they have sought the extreme isolation that nature demands in the lambing season. So the orphan is taken to a walled pen on the mountain, where it will remain until Tom finds a foster mother. Scotty watches anxiously

And now, me lad, you'd better take this bottle to the orphan in his lonely pen. He'll be hungry again by now, so don't loiter on the way

Remember where we left him? Well, go to it, old boy, and I'll keep supper for you. It's a long way after a gruelling day's work, but there you are

(Continued overleaf)

Though he has already had a hard day in the hills with his master, Tom Jones, wonder shepherd of Treorchy, Glamorgan, the sheepdog, Scotty, will set out across the moors with a bottle of milk for an orphan lamb left bleating in a lonely pen. These enchanting pictures, by ILLUSTRATED photographer Malindine, are dedicated to this, the cleverest dog in the world, who thoroughly enjoys his eventful life among the crags of the silent, timeless heather-covered hills

Scotty gets off, bottle held tightly, eager to get to that lonely mountain babe. Before him there lies a bewildering stretch of moor, dotted with stone pens and all around him lambs are bleating, but he goes straight to the orphan.

Up hill, down dale, over steep screes, walking with confidence and a sureness that comes of spending his days in rugged hills. Scotty presses on valiantly. Who said he wasn't the cleverest dog in the world? Well, isn't he?

Yes, he has arrived at the walled pen where the lamb has been waiting for him in faith that promise of new life. Safe from birds of prey and lonely, he will feed the loss of his mother. He is always ready for a call.

One result of the publicity from the film was that Dad was asked to appear at several cinemas with his dogs to give a 'Personal Appearance'. They were billed as:

'PERSONAL APPEARANCE - WELSH WONDER SHEPHERD'

Some fraudsters jumped on the band wagon and used his name to sell ointment for dogs. Dad was giving an exhibition in Birmingham and when he arrived on the field, there was a stall displaying huge posters – 'TOM JONES'S OINTMENT FOR DOGS'. It claimed to cure all diseases from Distemper to Mange. Dad actually bought a tin and tried it on his dogs. All it did was bring the dogs out in the most horrific skin rash!

His fame soon spread and he was approached to give exhibitions. He travelled country-wide with his pony and dogs. There are many amusing stories attached to these outings.

Travelling was difficult. He had no transport of his own, and it was not uncommon for him to travel many miles to a show on the back of his brother-in-law Howell's motor bike, - holding Scott, another dog Guide, and sometimes a lamb in between them.

Howell with Scott

On one occasion, when they were travelling to Birmingham, one of the dogs (there were two of them) jumped off the bike, and ran away. Despite an intensive search, they were unable to find the dog and they carried on to their destination without him. The show carried on with one dog and later on the other dog was found safe and well. The incident was recorded in a local newspaper by a cartoonist.

Money was very scarce and by now Mam and Dad had three daughters to support. Often there was no money for Dad to even pay the entrance fees for sheep-dog trials. To raise the money he often sold blackberries picked from the hedgerows. However, it appeared that where there was a will there was a way, and whenever possible, he managed to compete, travelling the length and breadth of the country with great success.

The South Wales Sheepdog Society bought a copy of the film and for several years it was shown after every meeting they held throughout South Wales. Many years later, Dad was really keen to get a copy of it, because none of his grandchildren had ever seen it. After several unsuccessful attempts to trace the film I contacted our M.P., Ann Clwyd, and asked if she knew how we could get a copy. Within three days of my request, she contacted me to say that she had traced the film. There were two nitrate copies in the Archives in London. She had asked for it to be put on to a video tape and we were able to purchase it. Our only regret was that Dad died two weeks before it arrived, so he never knew that we had found it. It would have meant so much to him. It has brought untold pleasure to us all as a family and we are so proud to know that 'Sheep Dog' will remain in the archives forever, alongside all the films of the great film stars.

ODEON

THEATRE——QUEEN ST CARDIFF

OUTSTANDING ADDITIONAL ATTRACTION !

Thurs. April 13th Fri. & Sat.

Supporting the latest United Artists Masterpiece

DUKE OF WEST POINT

With LOUIS HAYWARD and JOAN FONTAINE

at 1.20   3.47   6.25   8.55

" SHEEP DOG "

Mr. TOM JONES

OF TREORCHY.

(Champion Shepherd of Great Britain) and his three front-
running Sheep Dogs, who appear in the Film, will make

Personal Appearances on
the Stage at this Theatre

TWICE NIGHTLY AT

6.15 and 8.45

Programme for the Birmingham Floral Fete and Exhibition

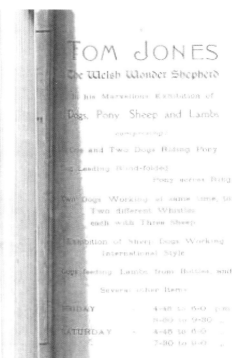

Cartoon from the Birmingham Gazette, 16th July 1932

Article from Ocean and National Magazine May 1939

This article appeared in a monthly magazine published by the Ocean Coal Company. The magazine contained articles contributed clerks at the company's collieries in South Wales. It contained news items, including reports of achievements of the company's employees, and family members. It was through the report of a clerk at the Parc and Dare Colliery that the film 'Sheepdog' was made.

"Shepherd of the Hills"

By C. J

Tom scents trouble from afar.

May, 1939.   *The Oscar National Magazine.*   Page 155.

roundings . . . "the daily routine among the crags of the silent, timeless, heather covered hills . . . within hearing of the curlew's whistle and the mechanical bleating of his flock . . . and possessing the deep-seated gentleness of the shepherd, well versed in the age-old lore of his calling." "Naturally," he said, "I

two photographers approached him and suggested that he might show them one or two of his "stunts." He readily complied, but was rather taken aback later that day when he saw pictures of himself and his faithful animals being retailed in the City of Salt a crown each. Added to this exploitation, he found two

A motherless lamb! All hands on deck!

her the work, but they make me think I am one of the shepherds of the Old Testament!"

From time to time, he has done a lot of public demonstrations, in both competition and exhibition, and is quite unaffected and guileless. For instance, a few years ago he was engaged to give a "show," with his pony and dogs, at Birmingham. At 8.30 in the morning

persons at the show busily engaged in selling what they described as "Tom Jones's Condition Powders," for dogs!

His dog, "Scot," which figures largely in the film, had been sold before the picture was taken, but Tom was able to borrow it for the occasion. And it is interesting to note that although the new owner was training the animal as

(Continued on Page 156).

THE WAR YEARS

1939 saw the outbreak of the Second World War. Dad became a Street Warden with the Home Guard in Treorchy. His job was to ride around the streets on his horse when the siren sounded making sure people were indoors. When the all clear sounded he would again ride around the streets to make sure everyone was safe.

The destruction left by the bombing, was something he found difficult to comprehend. He witnessed the bombing of Cwmparc on April 29th-30th 1941.

Mam often told a story about how he went up the mountain on the horse one morning, after there had been an attack on Treorchy and came home proudly carrying part of a German plane which had been shot down by a British plane. The German pilot had been killed. Mam could not believe how anyone would want to keep something of this sort as a souvenir, and was horrified. My father had the length of her tongue and was promptly told to get rid of it.

In 1942 Dad accepted the offer of the post of Head Shepherd at Parc Farm, Cwmparc. The farmhouse went with the job. It was a beautiful modern house, which had been built for the Colliery Agent. It had a bathroom with hot and cold running water, which was a luxury few working-class people had in those days. Mam was delighted and they moved in from Ystradfechan Cottages, Treorchy, straight away.

At the end of war in 1945, great celebrations took place. Mam and Dad hosted a party for the neighbours living alongside Parc Farm and many others who lived elsewhere in Treorchy and who had heard about the party. The whole street turned up to prepare the barn for the celebrations. It was painted with white lime, buntings were made and tables and chairs brought from houses in the neighbourhood. A piano took pride of place. There was even a stage erected, with curtains which were drawn together and then pulled back when the 'artiste' appeared. Many local residents participated in a 'Go as you please' competition, showing off their talents. Food was rationed, but somehow or other there seemed to be no shortage. There may have been some 'under the counter' black market practices in force!   It was a wonderful evening. The celebrations went on well in to the next day and were talked about for many months to come.

THE AWFUL TRUTH

In 1944, Nancy Jones, whom Dad had always believed to be his mother, died.   His eldest sister, Annie, asked him if he would accompany her to a solicitor's office in Pontypridd for the reading of Nancy's will.   It was here that he discovered for the first time, that he was not Nancy's son and that his birth mother was her sister, Mary. The shock of this discovery hit him very hard.   He could not believe that he had lived all his life in the same street as his mother, without knowing that he was her son.

Years later, when he was living at Tyle'r Fedw, Ynysybwl, he was asked by his bank to produce his birth certificate.   It was then, on obtaining a copy, that he discovered that although he had been known as Thomas Jones all his life, his birth certificate showed that he had been registered as Thomas Morgan (Morgan being his birth mother's maiden name). He had never been legally adopted by Nancy and Thomas.

From this time on, he had a yearning to find out who his natural father was. However, he never approached Mary about this and accepted that he would never know.

During the last years of his life, he and Mary became closer and for the first time in his life, in the year before she died, at the age of 89, he had a birthday card from her wishing him 'Happy Birthday Son'. He visited her regularly and he and I were the only persons present at her death. She was in bed in the front room, having been ill for quite some time. Several members of the family were in the kitchen. Dad and I were sitting talking to her, when she passed away peacefully. I have often reflected on the irony of that event, that the son she had given birth to, but never raised, was the one to be with her when she passed away.

CHAPTER 7

PENYLAN

In 1946 the Ocean Coal Company were selling all of their farms. The job of shepherd was made redundant. Dad was offered the tenancy of Parc Farm, Cwmparc, but a condition of the tenancy was the purchase of the sheep. He had no money and reluctantly he had to turn down the offer. The house where we lived in Treorchy was a modern house. Mam and Dad had been very happy living there, and had made several close friends in the area. They would have been quite happy to stay there for the rest of their lives, but they had no choice.

Dad was offered the tenancy of another farm - Penylan, a farm on the hills above Ynyshir in the Rhondda Fach. This was a big step; they had never been able to afford anything of their own, having previously lived in tied accommodation or rented rooms.

'Penylan' in 1946 with Llinos and Diana standing on the steps

Mam really didn't like the position of the farm, and hated the thought of living there, but they had little alternative but to accept. The farm was isolated with no proper access road - merely a dirt track, which could only be negotiated safely on foot. The house had no water and no electricity and the only means of heating and cooking was a coal fire with a side-oven. The house was cold and draughty. The only form of lighting was by oil lamps. On taking up the tenancy of Penylan, the first thing Dad had to do was to create some sort of access road, which would be suitable at least for horses, this still being the most common mode of transport for farmers in those days.

Life was hard to say the least. Mam and Dad both worked tirelessly on the farm, and, as was the case in those days everything had to be done by hand. There was no transport of any sort, - just a horse used for ploughing the fields, and any other work which could not be done by hand.

Although living conditions were grim, sometimes there was a humorous side to life. Mam was asked by a member of the family, if she could take in a relative who was down and out and had nowhere to live. Dai John Rees was a native of Cilgerran, a cousin of my grandmother Sarah Ann. He was by now a middle-aged man, who had been a loner all his life. He had worked as a general labourer on various farms, travelling from place to place. Mam and Dad, who would not see anybody without a home, agreed to let him come to stay. We didn't have much materially, but one thing we did have at the time was plenty of spare rooms, Penylan being a large three storey house.

Dai John would help Dad with odd jobs around the farm during the day, but found his way to the nearest pub every night usually returning home after the pub had closed. Because Mam and Dad had to get up early in the morning, they would go to bed before he would let himself in.

One night, Dai John didn't come home. As usual everyone had gone to bed so no one knew until the morning that he was missing. It had rained heavily during the night. Dad went to look for him, and found him fast asleep in a pool of water. He had obviously had 'one too many', had fallen over and been unable to get back up. Despite being soaking wet on a particularly cold night, fortunately he was a tough character and suffered no ill effect.

One of Dad's few leisure interests was to listen to boxing matches on the wireless. Because we had no electricity, one of the few luxuries we had was an old crystal set, powered by battery. On one occasion, there was a world title fight being broadcast. Dad was looking forward to listening to it, and after finishing his jobs came into the house and made himself comfortable in front of the fire. As seemed to be often the case, whenever there was something they wanted to hear, the battery on the wireless had run down and he could barely hear the commentary. By sheer chance, he discovered that by holding two wires at the back of the wireless and fitting them to a spare battery and holding them on in order to make some sort of contact, the volume increased. I can remember seeing Dai John, sitting in a chair, smoking his clay pipe and holding these wires for the duration of the fight. I still remember how funny it looked. Now and again, Dai John would move his fingers and the wires would come off, resulting in the wireless becoming silent. It seemed as if when the match got to an exciting part this would happen. Dad would be dancing up and down and Dai John would be frantically trying to get the wires back on. By the time they made contact again, he had missed the last few rounds of the match, and the commentator was giving the result!

Life at Penylan was never easy. Mam and Dad had to borrow money from a friend to buy some sheep and cattle, and it was a constant battle to make enough money to survive. After only a few months, Dad realised that he would have to look for some sort of paid employment, in order to supplement any income from the farm.

Fortunately he found work at Wattstown Colliery, just at the bottom of the hill from the farm. The manager arranged for him to work in the 'wagon repair' shop. This allowed him to work shifts, working around his daily work schedule on the farm.

Because they had very little money, they had to find the cheapest way of feeding the animals. They planted a field of swedes. The ploughing was done with the horse, but the task of sowing the seeds had to be done by hand. To do this, they used what was called a 'fiddle'. It was a violin shaped contraption, which had a leather strap which was placed around the neck.   From this hung a kind of sack in which the seeds would be placed.   There was a long 'bow' which was pushed backwards and forwards, releasing the seeds.   When the seedlings pushed through the ground, next came the laborious task of thinning the plants out. This job had to be done by hand. Mam and Dad would kneel down on the earth, painstakingly crawling their way up and down the rows, using an old canvas sack to kneel on. This job took days and days of back-breaking labour. Later on in life, Mam suffered with severe osteoarthritis of her knees. She often attributed this to that particular job.

The isolated, bleak situation of the farm became very evident when, in 1947, the snow came. This was to be one of the worst winters in living memory. We woke up one morning in January to find several feet of snow had fallen during the night. The high winds had caused it to drift, completely covering the entrance to the front door. Mam and Dad had to tunnel their way out of the house. They managed to make a pathway to the cowshed, where their few cattle were housed. There was only a limited supply of hay to feed the cows. Once this had been used, they were unable to get any further supplies. The road was impassable because of the depth of the snow which had frozen and become solid ice.

The only way they could get water for the animals to drink was by melting snow in buckets on the fire in the kitchen. With a yoke that straddled their shoulders they carried buckets of water to the cattle. Despite their best efforts several of the cattle died through lack of food and water. It was a heartbreaking situation watching the cows die and being unable to do anything to help them.

The natural instinct of sheep in bad weather is to find a place to lie which affords them some shelter. The fields were encircled with stone walls, and the sheep had sheltered against the walls when the snow had started to fall. Quickly the snow had drifted against the walls and had covered them. The snow froze the sheep's fleeces, making them heavy and impossible for them to get up and many were buried alive. The task of digging them out was impossible and the toll was not fully evident until the thaw came several weeks later. Dad walked around the fields and mountain trying to locate them. Over the years that he had worked as a shepherd, he had gained tremendous knowledge of sheep husbandry. The only way he was able to locate the sheep was by finding two little holes, which had pierced the surface of the snow. He knew that these had been made by the sheep's warm breath passing through their nostrils and up through the snow to the surface.

The experience of this cruel winter was devastating. Mam and Dad described it as 'Hell on Earth' and they knew that they could not face another winter there at Penylan. Dad asked the company if they could find him another farm to rent. Fortunately, a farm was becoming vacant in Ynysybwl and it was offered to them. They both went to see it and were happy to be going back to the village where Dad was born, and where they had lived when they were first married.

CHAPTER 7

Tyle'r Fedw

We moved into Tyle'r Fedw, Ynysybwl, in March 1948. With the help of a very understanding bank manager Mam and Dad were able to borrow money to buy some sheep and a few dairy cattle.

Once again, lady luck was not on their side. Whilst bringing in a load of hay from a field on the top of the mountain, Mam had been arranging the hay which Dad was passing up to her on top of the 'gambo', (a horse-drawn trailer which was used for collecting hay). She lost her balance and fell to the ground. In excruciating pain, and unable to move, both she and Dad knew that something serious had happened to her. They thought she was paralysed. Dad was in turmoil. He had no alternative but to leave her lying on the ground. There was nowhere to secure the horse and he had to leave it with the load of hay on the gambo, standing in the field. He ran down to the colliery, the nearest place where he could get help.

The manager of the colliery, after sending for the ambulance, arranged for some workmen and one of the first aid men to go up to the field. The road to the top field was very rough, and it was impossible for the ambulance to drive there. This meant that the men had to carry her down on a stretcher, a distance of at least a mile to the bottom of the farm road, where the ambulance was waiting to take her to hospital.

She was found to have fractured two vertebrae in her spine, and was told she was extremely lucky not to have been paralysed. She was put in a plaster cast, which reached from just beneath her chin to her knees. It was intended that the plaster jacket should remain in place for several months. However, it was a very hot summer and Mam found it unbearable to cope with. Never being one to be beaten, she was determined that this wasn't going to stop her from getting around. She persuaded my father over the following weeks to saw some of the plaster away using a hacksaw. Every couple of days she would ask him to saw a bit more until eventually the plaster only extended from the bottom of her neck to the top of her legs. She managed to walk and indeed work. The doctors in the hospital could hardly believe what they saw when she finally went to have it removed.

The following year, believing that things couldn't get any worse, they did. There was little grazing land for the cattle, so they decided to turn them out on to the mountain, where amongst the bracken there was a little grass. Almost the whole of their herd of cows died with bracken poisoning.

Financially things were very grim and once again Dad was forced to look for paid employment. The Colliery Manager, knowing how desperate his situation was, found him a job working underground. He hated the thought of going underground again, but he knew he had no alternative, and this was the only way they could survive. He worked night shifts, starting work at 9.30 in the evening and finishing at 6 in the morning. He hated it. He would walk home, where Mam would have filled a tin bath with water ready for him to have a bath. There were no pithead baths then and he would arrive home covered from head to toe in coal dust. Mam would get up for the day at 5am and her first job was to carry buckets of water from an outside tap (this being the only source of water) to a copper boiler in an outhouse. She would light a fire under the boiler, hoping that the water would be warm enough when Dad came home.

After bathing, he would have breakfast and then he and Mam would go straight out to milk the cows. The milk would then have to be taken down to the bottom of the farm, where it would be collected by the local milkman by 8 o'clock. After milking the cows and taking the milk down to the stand for collection, Dad would go to bed for a couple of hours, then get up and do whatever had to be done for the rest of the day. This included the evening milking before going to work at the colliery again in the night.

This went on for many months. It was heartbreaking for us to see him going each night to work knowing how much he hated being underground. I can clearly remember us standing outside the house, watching him going down the fields, all of us crying and wondering whether he would be safe.

HARD TIMES

Despite living in very difficult circumstances, Mam and Dad were determined that all their children would be given every opportunity to make the most of their lives. My mother was a very intelligent lady, who had been educated at Ferndale Secondary School. Unfortunately her parents, with a family of four children when my grandfather returned from the War, could not afford to keep Mam at school and she, together with her elder sister, Bessie, had to leave school in order to supplement the family income. In common with many men in the Rhondda Fach, my grandfather had been out of work for much of the 1920s and this increased the financial stresses on the young family. Both Mam and Aunty Bess found work as domestic servants in houses belonging to local professional families. Mam's older brother, Howell, worked in the local Colliery.

Mam had a beautiful Soprano voice, and, although money was very scarce my grandfather, who was extremely musical, ensured that she had voice training. She competed and won at eisteddfodau across South Wales. Amongst the prizes she won was a silver cup at the Ferndale Semi National Eisteddfod. Undoubtedly, she would have had a future in the singing world if circumstances were different and she had had the opportunity.

A story that always remains with me is that of my mother singing in the Workmen's Hall, Ferndale. The Hall was full to capacity; in the middle of her performance the electricity failed and the hall was immersed in darkness. Remaining calm, and being a 'true professional', she carried on singing. Despite this interruption, the audience were said to be so engrossed in the singing you could hear a pin drop. It was said that they hardly noticed the electricity cut.

When she was 16 years old, she joined a 'group of singers'. This was in 1926, the year of the General Strike. The miners had come out on strike for better wages and times were very hard. The group of young people walked for miles singing in towns as they went collecting money for the miners and their families.

The fact that she had been denied the chance to further her own education resulted in Mam and Dad being determined that their children would be given every opportunity to further their education however difficult things were for them. The sacrifices they made were huge, but they never once showed any sign of remorse and were so proud of our achievements. Of the three daughters, Nancy and Llinos became teachers after attending teacher training college and I became a shorthand typist after attending a local commercial college.

A GOOD TALE TO TELL

Although life was very hard and they had very little money, Mam and Dad always found time to care for others.

Tyle'r Fedw became a home to many young people who, for various reasons, needed some support. Although money was in short supply, no-one was turned away, and there was always a welcome and a hearty meal for anyone who needed it.

Dad was renowned for being able to tell a good story. He delighted in telling the youngsters wonderful ghost stories, one of which he swore was true - and witnessed when he was working as a young boy at Blaenllechau Farm. Boys of 16 or 17 years of age would be made to listen to all the gory details even though they were obviously frightened out of their wits, and just when he could sense their fright he would casually say to them "O.k. boys, time to go home now, it's getting late".

It's not difficult to imagine the scenario. Tyle'r Fedw was on top of the mountain, and very remote. There were no street lights and it would be very dark, particularly during the winter. Some of the boys related later in life how they would go out through the door quite casually pretending that they had been unaffected by the stories, but as soon as they were away from the farmhouse they would run as fast as their legs would take them, not stopping for breath until they reached their homes.

Dad was also a real practical joker. On one occasion, a young boy was staying at the farm (my sisters and I have often reflected on why we often had 'lodgers' staying with us). His mother and father were moving out of the village to Cowbridge, where his father had a job as a Bailiff. Mike didn't want to move so my parents agreed that he could stay with us. He was about l6 years old.

He wasn't renowned for being very brave, and this was the worst thing that my father could have discovered. If he went down to the village in the evening he was nervous about walking home in the dark. He would go to the local telephone box and ring my parents to tell them that he was on his way home. The local postmistress, Miss Evans, had to put all the telephone calls through. The exchange was in the post office. Ynysybwl was a village where everybody knew each other. One night Mike didn't have change on him (the cost of the phone call in those days was two pence). He picked up the phone and Miss Evans answered. He told her who he was and that he didn't have two pennies. She told him not to worry, she would put the call through, and he could put the money under the door the next time he passed there. Obviously the door she meant was the post office door. But misunderstanding Mike struggled to put the two pence under the door of the kiosk the following day!

Once Mike had telephoned Dad would then go outside the farmhouse and call him. Mike would then answer and Dad would stay outside until he got to the top of the hill. One night Dad thought he would play a joke on him. As soon as Mike rang he ran down the fields to the bottom of the hill and lay down alongside a wicket gate which he knew Mike would have to go through. Mike saw a body lying there alongside the gate, but because it was dark, he failed to recognise Dad. He decided that he would walk quickly past. As he passed, Dad got up. Mike saw this figure rising and picking up speed. The hill was about a l in 10 gradient. It was dark, but Mike decided not to hang around to see who it was. The faster he ran, the faster Dad ran behind him. By the time he got to Tyle'r Fedw he was so frightened and short of breath he was speechless. He turned to see Dad arriving right behind him, laughing wickedly and asking him what was the matter.

Another practical joke that Dad used to like to talk of was that of 'the headless lady'. There was a public footpath through the yard of Tyle'r Fedw. Some miners used to walk from Abercynon through the farm yard, taking a short cut to the Colliery.   Dad asked them one day, whether they had seen the 'headless lady'.   With a deadpan expression he told them about a ghost, a woman with no head, whom he had seen walking through the yard at night.   Although they did'nt know whether to believe him they were nevertheless just a little scared.   One night, he decided to test them to the limit.   He knew exactly at what time they would be walking through the yard and went out carrying a white sheet.   He stood by the door of the stable, and when he heard them coming he put the white sheet over his head.   He coughed to attract their attention and just walked slowly towards them.   They turned, saw him, and were so frightened they didn't stop to open the gate, but jumped over it.

FOUR HARD SEASONS

Each season of the year brought its different activities and problems. The spring was extremely busy, being the lambing season and the season when crops were planted.   When lambing was complete, the sheep were gathered for earmarking, dipping, and shearing.

Llinos and Diana feeding lambs

SHEARING

As was the custom neighbouring farmers all came to help with the shearing. The day would start as early as five o'clock, when the sheep would be gathered from the mountain and brought down to the farm. This was a wonderful event to witness. Dad's talents as a sheep-dog trainer really came into being. He usually had three working sheepdogs trained to work together, but all of whom had separate commands. Dad had a wonderful natural whistle, which could be heard across the valley. He would stand in front of the farmhouse and give the dogs the command to go. The sheep would be grazing on the mountainside, at least a mile or two distant from the farmhouse. The dogs would be sent one to the left, one to the right and another behind the sheep. With the most wonderful skill he would manage to bring the whole flock right down to the field alongside the farmhouse. It was wonderful to see the dogs working the flock, listening for the next command from Dad. With the utmost precision they would return to be rewarded with a pat on the back and a little tit-bit which he carried in his pocket (usually a piece of boiled pig's liver).

One farmer, Glyn, who lived at Pitwell Farm in Cilfynydd, was always the first to arrive. He used to ride over on his horse as early as he could in the morning. He would help Dad if it was necessary to gather in any "stragglers" - sheep which had somehow or other got away from the dogs. Once the sheep were brought down, they were held in pens in the field. The next task was to separate the ewes from the lambs. The lambs were never shorn. The noise of bleating when the ewes and lambs were separated was deafening. The ewes would then be brought down, perhaps 50 at a time, and put in a shed near to where the shearing was to take place.

Several men were involved in the shearing. There were the 'catchers', whose job it was to catch the ewes and bring them to the shearer. There were usually about ten men actually shearing, so the catcher's job was a busy one, making sure that as the shearer finished one sheep, the next one was there. Sometimes there was an air of competition between the shearers, seeing who could shear a sheep in the fastest time.

After shearing, someone had the job of 'marking'. This meant that a brand iron with the initials of the farmer was dipped in Raddle (a type of paint) and pressed firmly onto both sides of the sheep so that when they were turned out back onto the mountain they were easily recognisable.

One individual was put in charge of the 'medication' pot. If a sheep was nicked with a shears he would be called. He carried a pot that contained an ointment used to cover the wound to stop it becoming infected. Infestation with flies would, if left untreated, result in a non-healing maggot infested wound.

The final job in the process was to roll the fleeces. This was usually the job of the children and we would end up at the close of the day black and greasy and often more dirty than the shearers themselves. There was an art even to this job. The fleece was placed on a clean area of floor with the wool of the fleece facing upwards. It was carefully folded in from both sides, the tail being left until last. When the sides were folded, the fleece was carefully rolled until the tail was reached. This was then turned until it became almost like a rope and then tied around the fleece. There was a sense of satisfaction to see the neatly rolled fleeces piled up, ready to be transported to a lorry which would take them to the woollen mills.

Another job which seemed to land on the children was to keep the men supplied with cider. A cask of cider was ordered well in advance and kept in the pantry on a stone which was also used for salting the pigs after killing.

Often the shearing went on for a few days. When they had finished in one farm the shearers would congregate at the next farm on the following day; this went on for quite a few weeks until all the sheep had been shorn. The fun and camaraderie between the men was wonderful.

Of course, it wasn't just the shearing that was hard work. Mam would start preparing the food the day before. Huge joints of pork were cooked, together with umpteen plates of apple tart and piles of welshcakes. The men would arrive as soon as they could after milking their own cows or feeding their livestock. Some would come in for breakfast; bacon and eggs and fried bread. They would all come in for lunch. The top of the cooking range was always full of saucepans containing an array of different vegetables. The table would be laid and they would all sit around and eat until their appetites were sated. A few also stayed for tea.

The whole event was exciting although very hard work. It was the social event of the year for the farmers, a time when they all got together to exchange news from their individual farms.

The following day the task of earmarking the lambs before returning them to the ewes took place, and was followed by the dogs driving the sheep back up to the grazing areas of the mountain.

SUMMER – HAYMAKING

Nancy, Llinos and helpershaymaking at Tyle'r Fedw

Summer was the season for haymaking. To make the most of a dry day Dad would start mowing the fields at dawn. The horse was steered using long reins which reached to the back of the mowing machine. After every couple of rows it would be necessary to sharpen the knife in the mowing machine. The following day, whoever was available went out to turn the hay using wooden rakes. There would be several of us, one behind the other turning the hay over so that it would dry. This would have to be done again the following day and then, hopefully, it would be fit to harvest. The rows were pushed up with the rakes into piles, ready for the horse and gambo to come to collect. Someone would have to lift the hay with a pitchfork onto the gambo. In order for the hay not to fall off the cart it had to be placed in a certain way evenly across the length and breadth of the gambo, this being quite a skill in itself. When it was as high as it was possible to reach, a rope was tied underneath the gambo and then thrown over the top to another anchor point on the other side, and then back again another twice. This usually secured the load until it arrived in the hay barn.

The children were usually allowed to have a ride down on top of the hay. They were told to hold on to the rope and not to move. It was a thrilling experience. It felt like being on top of the world. One of the memories I have of this is having to lie as flat as possible in some parts, because there would be trees overhanging and we had to be careful that the branches didn't hit us off.

We always seemed to be lucky to have a lot of help, particularly during haymaking when young boys from the village used to come up. They seemed to really enjoy the whole experience. There was never any question of being paid (we didn't have any money) but they were quite satisfied when they were asked in to have supper at the end of the day's work. They always seemed to return on the following day - so they obviously enjoyed it.

AUTUMN

Autumn was also a very busy time, particularly for sheep farmers, as this was the time that lambs were taken to the market to be sold. This meant that all the sheep had to be brought down to the buildings in the farm yard, the lambs separated and 'sorted'. On arrival at the market the lambs were 'graded'. Any lambs that were not fat enough would be rejected by the grader and that meant that no subsidy would be paid for those lambs. The dealers then would hope to buy them at a lower price. Mam and Dad learnt how to grade them before sending them to market, as this saved a lot of time and money. They could tell by feeling the back of the lambs which ones were fat enough and which had to be kept for a further period. The cheques that came in from the sales of these lambs and the subsidies that were paid were a very welcome addition to their meagre income, and made the difference between survival or otherwise.

WINTER

Winter was probably the hardest season of all. Tyle'r Fedw is situated at the top of a steep hill and although glorious in the summer, because it seemed to be permanently in the sun (it was south facing), it was equally as bleak in the winter. The wind howled around the farmhouse, and there was very little shelter, particularly from rain or snow.

During the winter, the milking cows were brought in to the cowshed and not turned out until the spring. This meant that they would have to be fed twice a day with hay and what little concentrates could be afforded. The cowshed was cleaned out every morning after milking and again brushed after the evening milking was completed. The sheep grazed out all the winter, but this still meant they had to be checked every day to make sure they were alright.

LIFE AT TYLE'R FEDW

Home conditions were primitive. There was no running water in the house. The only water supply came from a tank, which collected rainwater from the roof of the house. Obviously if we had a dry spell, the supply would dry up. Dad then had to fill milk churns from either the houses who had a mains supply at the bottom of the hill or sometimes he would go to the colliery and fill them up from taps in the pithead baths. The toilet was outside and entailed quite a walk from the house (not a very pleasant experience in the dark). Paraffin lamps were the only source of light and we would have to carry these with us to light the way. The invention of battery operated torches was a huge improvement in later years. We had a tin bath, which was put into the wash-house where the copper boiler was situated. It was a cold room, but the heat from the fire underneath the boiler did help a little. We used to go to our Cousin Maureen's prefab to bath once a week, and that was sheer luxury.

The laundry work was hard. Hot water was carried in buckets from a boiler, under which a fire was lit in the outhouse, to a tin bath. Mam would then have to scrub the clothes using the old type of scrubbing board. The wet clothes were then taken to a huge mangle which had enormous wooden rollers that were turned using a side handle. Although it was very primitive, the clothes came out the other side as if they had been through a spin-dryer. Every spring, all the woollen blankets off the beds would be washed. My grandmother used to come over from Ferndale to spend a few days to help with the washing of these blankets, which were extremely heavy when wet. My sister, Nancy, from her first month's pay as a teacher, bought a washing machine for Mam. I can remember the day it arrived. Obviously it had to be filled up with buckets of cold water from the outside tap, but my mother thought it was wonderful. To put a switch on and heat the water without her having to light a fire under the boiler seemed like magic. There was a wringer on the top, and after the clothes had washed they would be passed through this to get most of the water out. We all spent the evening watching this new gadget. Although the washing machine was quite simple in today's terms to my mother it was a wonderful invention.

Nancy had a job at Hawthorn School. All the money she earned was given to my mother to help out with the bills, only keeping enough for her to pay for her bus fare to get to work and any other necessities. She learnt how to sew and made most of her clothes, which of course were then passed down to Llinos and eventually to me. Llinos also became a very good dressmaker and made her own clothes.

I never acquired these skills, and was much happier helping Dad on the farm. I loved the outdoor life and was never happier than when I was up to my knees in mud!

Although we had electricity in the house, the wiring left a lot to be desired. Electric shocks were part and parcel of life. Looking back we often think how fortunate we were that nobody was electrocuted.

Amongst all the other jobs my mother had, any decorating that was to be done became yet another one. She learnt how to wallpaper and although perhaps could not be considered an expert, there was no alternative. One memory I have is of my mother trying to put paper on the ceiling in the living room. She had to ask my father to help her. What a disaster! Mam was up on the step ladder holding the paper which was wet with paste. Dad was on the floor holding a sweeping brush with a clean cloth over it trying to sweep the paper along in front of my mother while she pressed it up in order for it to stick. This ended up with the brush going straight through the paper and draping itself over my father who was not blessed with the best of patience, and promptly screwed the whole piece into a ball and threw it away. Needless to say that was the only time Mam asked Dad to help her with any interior decorating. Although he was very talented in many ways decorating was certainly not one of his talents.

As we got older we took our turn, but we would always be very wary of papering the kitchen wall. The only electric socket in the kitchen was near the window. This was used for the washing machine, the iron and any other electrical appliance. It was a two-pin socket, and was obviously not geared up for modern appliances such as washing machines and irons. Nevertheless it worked. There was no such thing as 'earthing' the socket. This meant that when we would put the wet wallpaper on the wall we would often have an electric shock and we would have to turn the main switch off until we finished the papering.

Our cousin Maureen's husband, Billy, used to come up to help on the farm. He was quite a handy-man and whatever my mother or father asked him to do he would endeavour to do it. Mam became concerned about the electricity having no 'earth'. She asked Billy if he could help out. As always, he set about the task and put an earth wire from the tap into the ground outside. Not knowing anything about electricity, Mam was very grateful to Billy and she thought the problem was solved. Not so - every time anyone turned the tap on in the outhouse, they had an electric shock!

Dad, being the practical joker that he was, chewed this over in his mind. At the time a local policeman had to come to sign the stock book once a month. It was in this record book that any movement of animals was recorded, a requirement of the Government. One policeman who used to come was a fitness fanatic and was always telling us how he used to do a lot of weight training. He was obviously very proud of his muscles. Dad thought "I'll see how strong you are now." Knowing that the tap was 'live', he asked the policeman if he would do him a favour. He asked him if he could turn on a tap that was stuck suggesting, in a deliberately patronising manner, that they knew he was strong and would be able to do it. The policeman, only too keen to show off his strength, went out, rolled his sleeves up and placed both his hands on the tap ready to give it a good twist. It doesn't take a lot of imagination to know what happened next. In Dad's words "he almost lit up like a Christmas Tree". The policeman realised that my father had done this deliberately but fortunately saw the funny side of it - thank goodness.

The earth wire was removed from the tap, but no improvements were ever made to the wiring and somehow or other we survived without a major incident. Another unfortunate policeman was walking up to sign the stock book when my father came along in his van. He stopped and told the policeman to jump in. The van was in a poor state of repair to say the least and would certainly not have passed an MOT if there had been one in those days. The locks on the doors weren't working, so Dad tied them with a piece of baler twine tied to the handle of the window. When the police officer got in Dad started off and the policeman leant towards the door which promptly opened depositing him on the road, his helmet bouncing along behind them.

LLOYD

One boy who became part of the family was Lloyd Coombes. He started coming up to help on the farm when he was eight years old. Lloyd, who has the most remarkable memory, can talk in great depth and detail about things that happened during that time. He said that the first time he had met Dad was when he, his cousin and his brother had walked through the farm to reach the mountain, where they went to pick whimberries. This was quite common in those days and families spent hours on the mountains whimberry picking. On the way home, they were walking through the farmyard (there was a public path going right through the middle of the yard) when my father came over to talk. He asked Lloyd "Whose boy are you then?" When Lloyd told him, Dad knew the family very well. He asked Lloyd if he would like to come up to help around the farm. Lloyd said that somehow even on that first meeting, he felt that there was something 'special' about Dad. The next day was a Sunday. Lloyd had been to chapel and, still in his Sunday best clothes, he went up to the farm. He said the first job Dad gave him to do was to carry a bucket of coal from the coal house into the house. Apparently, my mother said "Don't ask him to do that – he's in his best clothes", but nevertheless he did. He said he was so small he could hardly carry the bucket even when it was empty let alone when it was full of coal, but somehow he managed it and that was the beginning of many happy years for Lloyd at Tyle'r Fedw. His mother was plagued by ill-health and died when he was just 10 years old; Lloyd spent most of his life until he married as part of our family. Although there were many boys and young men over the years that spent a lot of time with us, there was something special about Lloyd, and he and Dad had an almost father and son relationship.

Some of the tales Lloyd can tell about those days are so funny. He remembers Tyle'r Fedw as always being warm and with the best heating system he has ever experienced. He attributes this to the fact that the coal fires which were lit in the kitchen Rayburn and the living room were always blazing. Dad had his own way of lighting fires which Lloyd soon learnt. He would place the paper and sticks in the fire grate and add some paraffin or diesel before setting a match to it. Lloyd remembers never having any eyebrows during his childhood, as the flames would shoot out and singe them. The Rayburn had quite a small opening for the fire, and Dad loved to see a glowing fire. He used to throw a bucket of coal on until the whole opening was full. The heat was incredible. We never needed central heating because the heat warmed the whole of the upstairs. The sides of the Rayburn had burnt away, and the actual metal was protruding. How we never had a serious fire remains a mystery

Lloyd remembers the milking machine being installed and how Dad was so proud of it. Dad impressed upon Lloyd the importance of the cleaning routine of the pipes etc. He said that in the first week the machine would be dismantled after milking and cleaned thoroughly with brushes etc. This was not a practice that was maintained however - after a very short time a quick dip in the water would suffice.

Lloyd remembers how two young boys started coming up to help. There was almost an induction ritual for any newcomers when they would be told to do something which was completely nonsensical. He told the boys that there was a special key which had to be placed in the ear of the cows and turned before any milk would come out. He said that for quite a while, he would put a key in the cows' ears and pretend to turn it before putting the milking machine on. The boys thought that this was true and were fascinated every time he did this. I don't know whether he ever told them the truth or whether the poor souls went through life believing this.

Another event of major importance was the delivery of the first tractor. Lloyd remembers having to go down to the bottom of the hill to collect the tractor because the delivery lorry was unable to get up the hill that led to Tyle'r Fedw. He was given the job of driving the tractor up to the farm. Dad never considered for a minute that perhaps he should have had some driving lessons first - he was only about 12 at the time!

Many youngsters had their first taste of driving, be it the van or the tractor, up at the farm. Dad never seemed to be worried about the fact that they had never driven before and simply told them how to turn on the key, put their foot on the clutch, engage the gear and off they would go. Thinking back to those days, we often wonder how on earth no-one had a serious accident. Health and Safety Departments would have had a field day, had they been in existence then.

Lloyd became a machine-driver. He was employed by a firm who had responsibility for maintaining the coal tip on Lady Windsor Colliery. His expertise at driving was put to good use when one day Dad was driving the tractor cutting hay on a particularly steep field. At the bottom of the field, there was a wire fence. At the other side of this fence is a steep Quarry. Dad had got off the tractor to clear a blockage in the mowing machine. He had not put the brake on properly and the tractor started running away. He tried to jump out of the way, but his coat got caught in the mowing machine and dragged him down with it. The tractor went straight through the wire fence and was balancing over the top of the quarry. He couldn't release himself. Someone from Other Street had seen what was happening and contacted Mam who was in the house. She didn't know what to do, but thought of Lloyd. She rang the Colliery. They got a message to him and he came with his machine to pull the tractor back. The two front wheels of the tractor were suspended over the edge of the quarry. Lloyd said it was the most frightening experience he had ever had and only through his skill as a machine driver was a tragedy averted. Somehow or other he managed to pull the tractor back, although at one stage he thought he was going to go over the quarry as well! Whenever we get together, we have a real laugh, listening to the tales that Lloyd tells. He says that the worst decision he ever made was to decline the many offers that Mam and Dad made him to live with us permanently. He has wonderful memories of the years he spent with us and loves to reminisce about them whenever we meet.

Girls were not exempt from helping at the Farm. Lynne Peart was a young girl who lived in Thompson Street in Ynysybwl. Her father, Rowley, had an allotment at the foot of Tyle'r Fedw. He kept a horse and was a very keen gardener. Lynne started coming up to help on the farm from a young age. She and her friend Irene Durham spent an awful lot of time there. Lynne was a real outdoor girl and enjoyed all aspects of farming. She had a wicked sense of humour and she and Dad got on really well. She would help with the cows, sheep and pigs and was rarely seen without a pair of wellies and would do anything that was asked of her. Tragically Lynne was killed riding her horse from Ynysybwl to Abercynon.

NOT THE BEST OF DRIVERS!

Dad was a notoriously bad driver - he never really got to grips with the reality that he was supposed to drive on the left-hand side of the road. He was renowned in the village for straying on to the path of oncoming traffic. He was very short, and found it more comfortable to stand up when he was driving the tractor as he had a better view. This was how he drove on the main road in Ynysybwl, raising his hand in greeting to anyone he passed and often turning his head round to see them as well.

Always ready to give somebody a lift, he would pull up at a bus stop if he saw someone waiting for a bus. Apart from the smell that was always prevalent in the van (silage, manure etc.) the journey was often described by passengers as being the most terrifying of their lives. One lady to whom he had given a lift to Pontypridd said that when she got out, she thanked him for the lift but added "If you ever see me again Tom - please don't stop - I'll catch a bus".

Mary Cresci, who owned the cafe in Ynysybwl, was a dear friend of mine. Dad used to go to the cafe on a Friday morning during the latter years of his life. He would sit with two other men, who were of the same vintage and always lived in the village, talking about old times. Mary used to join them. She used to hate anyone coming into the shop, because she would have to leave them to go to serve and would miss part of the conversation. Dad had a wicked streak in him and would say to Mary "I think I'll try a couple of losins". Mary had shelves full of sweet bottles. He would ask her if he could try one to see if he liked it. Eventually, having gone through quite a few of the jars, he would tell her he was full up now and he had decided not to buy any sweets after all. This was a standing joke between them. On one occasion, I was standing for election to the local council. On the day of the election, Dad went to the shop and said to Mary "Have you been to vote for our Diana?" Mary said she couldn't go because she had to stay in the shop. Dad asked her assistant if she would look after the cafe for him to take Mary up to vote in the van. She did. Whenever she talked about it later, she said that she never thought she would see the cafe again. The polling booth was only in the next street, but she said when they were going down the road Dad was waving to everyone, not looking where he was going, and the van veering towards the opposite side of the road. There was a bus coming and the driver waved at him telling him to get over. Dad said "Merry Christmas to you too". He turned to Mary and said "Did you see that idiot then Mary?" Mary was too shocked to speak. She didn't go out very often, and said that it was the experience of a lifetime, but she wouldn't want to go out again in a hurry.

SOME GOOD TIMES

Because of the continual shortage of money, we had to become as self-sufficient as possible. We always kept a pig or two, which my father killed about once a year. He had a licence for slaughtering animals and would often be asked to go to farms in the neighbourhood for this purpose. He was skilled at cutting animals up into joints and had learnt how to cure the bacon. The house always had flitches of bacon and hams hanging up from hooks in the oak beams in the living room. Whenever visitors came, my father would cut a good portion from one of the hams for them to take home with them, usually with a dozen fresh eggs to accompany it.

My mother would make trays of faggots. There was nothing wasted. The pigs' trotters would be boiled and the head used for making brawn. We kept chickens, and every Friday night my mother and I would carefully wrap each egg up in newspaper (to prevent them from breaking, there being no such thing as egg boxes in those days), place them in a shopping bag and make the journey to Ferndale on buses. There my grandparents would give me a list of customers to whom the eggs were to be delivered. My grandfather kept a strict record of who had paid and who owed. If they didn't pay for one week, the egg supply would be stopped. We used to catch a bus from Ynysybwl at about half past five on a Friday night arriving in Ferndale at about half past six. We always left Ferndale on the nine o'clock bus, arriving home about ten o'clock and then having to walk up to the farm. The small income we had from these eggs became very important.

Our income was meagre. We used to have a milk cheque once a month for about £20 and in the autumn, the lambs were sold. We were paid for the fleeces. We had a few sows, which were kept for breeding and the litters were sold, which brought in some money. After paying the bills for feedstuffs and all other expenses, there was very little money left to spend.

My mother wanted us to learn to play the piano, and we all had piano lessons. I started having lessons with a man in the village. When I went to the Commercial College, in Rhydyfelin, I began having lessons with a lady who lived in Church Village. I paid for my lessons by taking a dozen eggs to school with me. I would have to carry them around all day and then catch a bus to the lesson in Church Village and then back to Ynysybwl.

Although we had very little materially, there was always a plentiful supply of good food and I still remember getting up from bed in the morning, going downstairs knowing that there would be a cooked breakfast of bacon and eggs keeping warm on the Rayburn cooker in the kitchen. Even better was walking home from school, which was at least a mile from the village, knowing that my mother would be there waiting for me, - the house, although poor, being cosy and warm with a meal waiting. This, even as a child, seemed to make up for the material things we didn't have.

The farm seemed to be a haven for so many people and despite the fact that, at times, they could barely exist themselves, their door remained constantly open to anyone who needed it. My mother was an extremely good cook and even to this day people living in the village say they have never tasted blackberry tarts and Welsh cakes the like of those that she made.

Lloyd says he never understood how my mother always managed to find a good meal. He said it didn't matter how many people came, she would always find plenty for them to eat. When she made Welsh cakes she seemed to make enough to feed the whole village

Although there was very little time for leisure activities of any sort, one thing that happened every year was a party for the family which usually took place on New Year's Eve. Relatives from Ynysybwl and also from Ferndale in the Rhondda came. The night was one of family fun, traditional games, a good buffet meal and drinks (probably a cask of cider). Everyone was welcome and sometimes it was known for fifty people or more to turn up. Dad's usual party piece was to perform, with great seriousness, a monologue, 'The Burial of Sir John Moore'.

On one of these occasions Haydn Seymour picked up a shotgun which was always kept in the living room and used occasionally to shoot foxes. He lifted up the gun and pulled the trigger back to look up the barrel. He could see that the barrel was blocked and realised that there was a wad of pound notes stuffed into it. Dad had pleasure in hiding the occasional note somewhere where he thought Mam wouldn't find it. Although he never wanted money to buy anything for himself, this hiding of money was a peculiar habit of his. Haydn called out loud, "What's this Tom?" Mam was quick to relieve Haydn of the money and Dad didn't put it there again.

On another occasion when they lived in Glynderwen, he hid some money under a bedside lamp, next to his bed. It was money that one of the children had given him for tack for their horses. What he didn't realise was that the base of the lamp was glass and the money was clearly visible and spotted by Mam when she went to clean the bedroom! He was relieved of that as well!

THEIR OWN HOME AT LAST

When we lived in Ynyshir, Mam used to buy her groceries from the local grocer, Mr Griffiths. Dad had always been a very heavy smoker. Of course this added to the shortage of money that they had, and because he was very dependent on cigarettes, he was bad tempered if he didn't have any. Cigarettes were scarce. Nancy, being about 16 at the time, had gone down to the village to see if she could buy some but there were none available. She came back home and when she told Dad that there were no cigarettes there; he got into a temper and walked down to the village himself. The only cigarettes he could find were some 'Turkish' brand, called 'Pashas'. Apparently one had to be brave to smoke these. The smell was horrendous. He decided to go to Ferndale to see if he could borrow some cigarettes from his brother in law, Howell. He caught a double-decker bus and found a seat on the upper deck. He lit up a cigarette and he said that as soon as he started smoking it, the people that were sitting there started to cough and before they went very far, he was the only one left upstairs. Everyone else had moved downstairs. As desperate as he was to smoke, he couldn't face another one of these and the rest of the packet was thrown away!!

When we moved to Ynysybwl, Mr. Griffiths, the grocer, asked Mam if she would continue to trade from him. She agreed and he used to travel to Ynysybwl by bus once a week, and carry the groceries up to the farm.

Dad's one pleasure had been his cigarettes. He had always been a very heavy smoker. Essentially he was a chain-smoker, lighting one cigarette after another. The weekly grocery delivery always contained 200 Woodbine cigarettes. It was when an insurance agent, on one of his visits to collect premiums for a policy, suggested that they could take out an endowment policy that Dad decided to give up. He had initially laughed at the suggestion, saying that they would never be able to afford the premiums. Mam said that if he was to give up smoking the money they were spending on cigarettes would pay the premium for the endowment. He decided there and then that this made a lot of sense. They took out the Policy, and he knew once they had signed on the dotted line, he would not be able to afford to smoke again. In fifteen years, the endowment policy matured, and at the same time the N.C.B. was selling Tyle'r Fedw. The proceeds of the endowment allowed them to buy the farm. For the first time in their lives they owned their own home. Although this was quite late in their lives, it was a wonderful feeling and they were so proud of their achievement.

CHAPTER 8

GLYNDERWEN

At the age of 70 Dad decided to retire and he sold most of the sheep. At the same time, the former colliery manager's house, Glynderwen, at the foot of the hill, was being sold by the NCB. This was a significantly grander house than Tyle'r Fedw and one of the finest houses in the village. The N.C.B. had put the house up for tender and Mam and Dad decided to try to purchase the house. Their tender was accepted.

Apart from Parc Farm in Cwmparc, where they had lived for some years, this house was the only house in which they had lived that had modern conveniences – running hot water, a bathroom and indoor toilet, etc. Dad thought it was wonderful to be able to have a shower every day.

However, despite appreciating these advantages, there were regrets. When they first moved to Glynderwen Mam was not happy. In contrast with the situation of Tyle'r Fedw, she felt Glynderwen to be 'closed in'. Although the farm was on top of the mountain she could always go out on to the front and see movement. The view from the farm was superb and although it was quite remote, she was able to see cars and buses etc. down in the village; she never felt lonely. When they moved to Glynderwen, although it was adjacent to the Colliery, there was a silence and lack of outlook that she couldn't get used to.

THE PONY CLUB

Life changed at Glynderwen when I started a Pony Club in the village. My own children all had horses as did those of my sister Llinos. I felt that there was a call for a Pony Club which the children could attend in order to learn the pleasure that could be achieved by having company to ride out with. The first meeting of the Pony Club took place in the paddock of Glynderwen. 20 children with their horses turned up. From that day on the house was never empty. The children used to meet there and go for rides up in the forestry and around the fields of the farm. Mam and Dad were never happier. They had company every day. The parents of the children used to come up to help them with the horses, and this usually ended up with them volunteering to do odd jobs around the farm. It was like the good old days all over again.

One man, Eddie, who had started coming up to the farm when he was quite young but had stopped when he got married, started coming to

Glynderwen. His son had a pony and joined the pony club. Eddie became a valued member of the pony club.

One day, I had a call from someone who lived in the village. They said that a sheep and a lamb had wandered down the quarry face and were stuck on a ledge and couldn't get back up. This happened quite often and Dad took it all in his stride. He would go to the top of the quarry, tie a rope to a tree and to himself and let himself down to where the sheep were. He would tie another rope around the sheep and whoever was helping him, would pull the sheep up to safety.

The lady who telephoned me that day lived in Other Street, situated opposite the quarry face. She explained that they didn't ring Dad, because he was too old now to go down the quarry himself and they had phoned the RSPCA who said they would send someone over. The RSPCA officer saw the sheep and decided that it was too risky to attempt to save them. He went to see Dad and told him that he was going to send for a marksman to shoot the sheep off the ledge. Dad was horrified. The reason for this was that if left there, the sheep would die of starvation and therefore suffer. He told him in no uncertain terms that nobody was going to shoot any of his sheep and he would go down and get them himself. The RSPCA officer was terrified and tried his best to dissuade Dad, but he would have none of it. With the help of Eddie he went to the top of the quarry, tied the rope to the tree and let himself down effecting the rescue. Dad was 77 years old at the time. He was presented with a Bronze Medal for Bravery by the RSPCA. Unfortunately Eddie died before he could receive his award for assisting in the rescue. The RSPCA officer became a regular visitor when he was in the area, and would call in for a cup of tea. He said he had so much respect for my father.

At the ceremony, when he was presented with his medal, it was commented that it was most unusual for someone to receive awards for virtually the same act of bravery almost 50 years apart - silver in 1931 and bronze in 1980.

● 100 foot cliff scale to save sheep

'Bwl farmer Tom to get bronze medal for rescue

By JEAN PARRY

Farmer Mr. Tom Jones

Another family often reminisce about what they consider as very special days to them. John, one of the parents of the children in the pony club had a heart attack. He was unable to return to work, and found life very difficult. He started going to Glynderwen to see to his daughters' horses every morning after the children had gone to school. He would be called in to the house to have a meal, and very often spent most of the day with Mam and Dad who became very fond of him. Both he and his wife are certain that his time spent in Glynderwen had a big part to play in his recovery. His wife would get anxious because John was a long time and she would ring Mam. She would assure her that he was fine and this would put her mind to rest.

In these years at Glynderwen, Mam and Dad were never lonely. Glynderwen was a hive of activity. Pony Club Meetings were held in the front room, with as many as thirty people attending. The catering for the annual Gymkhana was done by the mothers of the children. All the sandwiches were prepared and the food, which was bought in the previous week, was stored in the front room. Mam was in her element and enjoyed every minute of it.

Many of the pony club children spent much of their time during school holidays and after school in the summer at Glynderwen. They all helped with little jobs around the farm which Mam and Dad still owned, although Dad had retired.

Mam and Dad had kept a few sheep and there was nothing the children liked better than going 'shepherding' during lambing time, my father accompanying them on horseback although by now he was in his seventies. Their reward was a meal when they returned, followed by freshly cooked Welsh cakes. Most of the children who went to the Pony Club called Mam and Dad Mother Gu and Father Gu (which is how they were known to all their grandchildren).

I recently met with Melissa, one of the girls who had kept their horses at Glynderwen. She reminisced about those days and said that they were the happiest of her life. She said how she used to go out with Dad and a couple of the other children shepherding, and would be out all day, returning home tired and very hungry. They would all be welcomed into the house for tea. Melissa said she can still remember the taste of those Welsh cakes. She remembers one day when they had been earmarking lambs (cutting the tops of the ears off) which was how farmers identified their own sheep then. She remembers that she used to wear a yellow weatherproof coat and on this day the coat was covered in blood. She walked home, wearing her riding boots and coat, down through the village where people were staring, wondering what on earth she had been doing. She says how different things are today. Young girls would not dream now of walking down through the village wearing a blood stained coat and riding boots. It just wouldn't be 'cool'.

An early meeting of the Pony Club c 1976: Dad (with his favourite jumper complete with holes!), Mam, 'Guide' (Dad's dog) and grandchildren Bethan and Siriol Lauder (Llinos's children); Beverley, Karen, Helen and Nicola Wilson (Diana's children).

There seemed to be a constant flow of visitors to Tyle'r Fedw and Glynderwen. One of the things they would often ask was for Dad to show them his dogs working. He would take them out to the barn, where he had as many as four dogs (all working sheepdogs). He would tell the dogs to sit. He would then whistle to each dog in turn and they would come, one at a time to him, the others remaining motionless until their own individual whistle was given. The control he had over them was remarkable. Dad would then give a display of gathering the sheep, often working the three or four dogs at the same time.

Although Dad had officially 'retired', and had sold most of his sheep, he kept a small group of young ewes so that he could train his dogs. These bred and eventually he had a small flock again. He bought a dog, which looked almost identical to Scot that was used in the film. He named him Spot. He taught him to do exactly the same things as he had trained his other dogs to do, and soon had him leading a pony, feeding a lamb with a bottle and various other things. Groups of schoolchildren used to come up to see the dogs and ponies performing. He used to train his ponies to do some 'fun' things. For example he would ask them questions and they would shake their heads for 'no' and nod for 'yes'. He would get the pony to lie down to pretend he was asleep. One of the favourite tricks, with the children was when he would ask the pony how old he was. He would paw the ground with his foot, until the appropriate number was reached.

In 1976, the local newspaper approached Dad to ask if they could come up to interview him and take some photographs. It was the Pontypridd Observer. Dad was now 75 years old, but still as capable of training his animals as he had been 50 years before.

He was often asked by the head teacher of Trerobart Primary School to go to the school to give a talk to the children. He would take a young lamb with him, and his dogs, and this was very popular with the children, especially when the dogs would feed the lamb with a bottle. He also visited elderly people in the locality who were unwell. He would take the lamb for them to see and they loved this.

These were very happy days, and have provided my children and my nieces and nephews with the most wonderful memories. One of the things they often say when reminiscing, (which they often do), is that they never remember Mam shouting at them despite the fact that there was sometimes a houseful of children at Glynderwen. There were very few nights during the long summer holidays when there weren't four or five children sleeping there. Mam took it all in her stride. She literally had the patience of Job.

"Tom has a marvellous way with animals

Pony answers questions – and dog feeds lambs with milk

Story:
Jean Parry

Pictures:
Paul Rose

WITHOUT A shadow of a doubt Ynysybwl's richest man is 75-year-old farmer Tom Jones.

Tom, whose tremendous character is revealed in his face.

Spot's talent

Cruel? — rubbish!

Changes his age

We enjoyed it

An article from the Pontypridd Observer, 1976

THE FINAL YEARS – OUR LEGACY

Passport photos for a holiday to Belgium

Eventually, age took its toll and Dad developed a mild form of dementia. Although this was quite difficult for Mam to cope with, being the person she was, she did. When he was eighty two years old, Dad became ill. Mam, Llinos, Nancy and I nursed him at home until he died. Glynderwen was sold and Mam moved to live with Llinos.

The following is part of a letter written to my mother by friends of the family at the time of Dad's death. I think it sums up what people thought of both Mam and Dad and I thought is a fitting tribute to them both.

'To know Tommy was to love him, and it was a great privilege to us to be welcomed by you both at your home. We enjoyed our visits to you very much and have talked many times of the pleasure and happiness we had there with you. Tommy was like no one else and his sense of humour and his stories have brightened the lives of all the people that he met. He was a great little Welshman and he will be remembered by all his friends with great respect and affection. May God help you in these very dark days of hiraeth and I am sure that it will be a comfort to you to know that so many people are thinking of you in your sad loss – God Bless you and your girls.'

Mam died in 2003 at the age of ninety-three. Fortunately, we had the privilege of being able to nurse both Dad and Mam at home and they died, surrounded by their loving family.

On the following pages are two poems that I wrote in the days following their deaths. We consider ourselves very fortunate to have had such wonderful parents, who were selfless and gave their all to their children, grandchildren and great-grandchildren. We all have very precious memories of them. For what more could we ask?

MAM

A gentle, kind and loving mother
Beyond compare with any other
You gave us your love till the end of your days
You showed us that in so many ways

Your life was not easy, you struggled hard
To give us the best and all that you had
You went without and never complained
The selfless sacrifices you always made

We learnt to follow your lessons in life
Be honest, work hard, and cope with strife
You set us the standards that you lived by
No greed, no envy – not to question why

Your joy in life was easy to see
The love you gave to your family
From babies to adults – you loved us all
No troubles too big – you shared them all

We loved you so much and always will
The memories you left are with us still

God bless you and keep you safe in his arms.

Diana.

MY DAD

His face bore signs of a life that was hard
The lines deep-seated, his skin scorched and scarred
His eyes had a glint – they sparkled and shone
Belying the worries – long since gone

His hands were rough, well worn, abused
Cut and cracked, unprotected – well used
He gave of his all, not seeking reward
His lived as a serf – but also a "Lord"

All his life he struggled to make ends meet
Ploughed the fields with horses- gathered corn and wheat
He had contentment – could he ask for more?
Not for him any yearning to leave his home-shore

As he tended his sheep – his dogs at his side
His life was tranquil, his heart full of pride
His death was peaceful – he just fell asleep
Leaving us, his loved ones, alone to weep

His epitaph must surely be:
Thank you God for his life and what he meant to me.

Diana.